STONEWALL KITCHEN
WINTER CELEBRATIONS

STONEWALL KITCHEN
WINTER CELEBRATIONS

Special Recipes for Family and Friends

BY JONATHAN KING, JIM STOTT & KATHY GUNST

Photographs by Jim Stott

CHRONICLE BOOKS
SAN FRANCISCO

Library of Congress Cataloging-in-Publication Data:

King, Jonathan.
  Stonewall Kitchen winter celebrations : special recipes
for family and friends / By Jonathan King, Jim Stott,
and Kathy Gunst ; Photographs by Jim Stott.
     p. cm.
  ISBN 978-0-8118-6868-6 (hardcover)
  1. Cookery, American. I. King, Jonathan. II. Gunst, Kathy.
III. Stott, Jim. IV. Stonewall Kitchen (Store) V. Title.

 TX715.K528 2009
 641.5973—dc22

                        2008043043

Manufactured in China

Designed by Katie Heit
Prop styling by Andrea Kuhn
Food styling by Catrine Kelty

Ka-Me Rice Crunch Wasabi Crackers are a registered trademark
of Schaffer, Clarke & Co.

10 9 8 7 6 5 4 3 2 1

Chronicle Books LLC
680 Second Street
San Francisco, California 94107

www.chroniclebooks.com

DEDICATION
To our mothers and grandmothers
that passed down these delicious holiday traditions.
—J.K. and J.S.

To my family, past and present.
Thank you for the rituals and the love.
—K.G.

ACKNOWLEDGMENTS
Many thanks to our editor, Amy Treadwell, and to all those at Chronicle Books
who helped make this such a beautiful book. Thanks to Doe Coover, our agent,
for making this all happen.

Thanks to our talented crew who helped with the photography:
food stylist Catrine Kelty, prop stylist Andrea Kuhn, assistant food stylist
Kim Gallagher, and photography assistant John McNeil.
Special thanks to Jessica Thomson, who helped shape and perfect the recipes.

TABLE OF CONTENTS

INTRODUCTION

Are you a holiday person? You know what we're talking about. The holidays divide the world into two types: those who love them and those who wish the calendar would magically skip ahead to January 2, so they could get on with life.

TYPE ONE: It's November and the days are getting darker and colder. You feel the sense of anticipation everywhere. You get out the good china, plan holiday feasts, and start to cook. You fill the kitchen with the comforting, buttery scent of your favorite cookies and pies baking in the oven. You can't wait to start shopping and find the perfect something for everyone important in your life. The little kid in you is awake and alive—it's holiday time. Life is good.

TYPE TWO: It's November and the days are getting darker and colder. You can feel that sense of dread creeping into your bones. Family and friends are calling and making plans. The radio and television play those insidious holiday tunes over and over. You check the Internet to see how much it will cost to run away but you know, no matter where you are, the holidays will prevail. So you start to make lists. One list has everyone's name on it next to a gift idea. Then there's the list of groceries to buy for all those holiday meals. And the list of chores to do before the family arrives—buy the tree, find the menorah, put up the wreath, stack the firewood, get replacement bulbs for the holiday lights. On and on it goes.

Take a deep, long breath. Whether you're type one or type two, there is a way to make it through all these winter celebrations and truly enjoy the season. The key is to know your limits and do some good planning and organizing before things get too hectic.

Stonewall Kitchen Winter Celebrations can help. There are more than forty-five recipes here that can make any holiday or winter meal something to remember. We kept a keen eye on creating recipes and menus that are celebratory; ones that will dazzle, but also can be prepared ahead of time so that the last-minute details—and stress—are kept to a minimum.

You'll find no-fail recipes for the big meals. We've included the holiday classics, but given them all a new, interesting, and subtle twist. Roast turkey (page 71) is basted with fabulous garlic butter and stuffed with Cranberry-Pecan

"TAKE A DEEP, LONG BREATH. WHETHER YOU'RE TYPE ONE OR TYPE TWO, THERE IS A WAY TO MAKE IT THROUGH ALL THESE WINTER CELEBRATIONS AND TRULY ENJOY THE SEASON."

Stuffing. There's a Standing Rib Roast Studded with Garlic (page 55) and our Holiday Ham (page 77) is glazed with maple syrup, cloves, and marmalade. We've got a no-fail Beef Tenderloin with Horseradish Crust, Roasted Potatoes, and Garlic (page 53), fork-tender Brisket with Winter Vegetables (page 59), and a Rack of Lamb with Pistachio-Garlic-Herb Crust and Roasted Cherry Tomatoes (page 65).

But we also included dishes for non-beef eaters: fabulous Baked Pasta with Roasted Wild Mushrooms in a Creamy Thyme Sauce (page 81) and a decadent Roast Salmon

and Scallops with Orange-Champagne Beurre Blanc (page 79).

You'll find recipes for every-day winter meals to share with family and friends, everything from Butternut Squash Soup with Curried Pecans, Apple, and Goat Cheese (page 28) to fabulous winter salads (pages 19, 22, and 25), Butterflied Lamb with Swiss Chard–Pine Nut–Parmesan Stuffing (page 62), and warming Osso Buco with Orange Gremolata (page 67).

There are plenty of interesting side dishes (always everyone's favorite part of a holiday feast), like a trio of unusual mashed vegetable combinations: Alabaster: Mashed Potatoes and Turnips (page 86), Orange-Scented Mashed Butternut Squash (page 89), and Mashed Parsnips and Pears (page 87). We've got Sharp Cheddar and Herb Popovers (page 107), an orange-kissed cranberry sauce (page 108), and a fabulous, silky custard made from roasted garlic, herbs, and Parmesan cheese (page 100). And, of course, cookies, cakes, pies, and more (see Desserts, page 113) to top it all off in celebratory fashion. Check our menu ideas (pages 135–139) for tips on how to put it all together.

We've also included a small collection of recipes that make fabulous gifts. For us, the holidays are all about spending time with family and friends *in* the kitchen. We prefer chopping to shopping. A gift of homemade buttercrunch (page 114), Curried Maple Pecans (page 49), or Orange-Ginger Shortbread (page 122) is better than a tie or new perfume any day. Check out all our Gifts from the Heart of the Kitchen ideas on page 117.

Try to keep in mind that all of this—the lists, the cooking, the cleaning, the shopping, the gift wrapping—is supposed to be about sharing, love, and enjoyment. These are all ways we have to tell the people in our lives that we care. We cook and we shop and we wrap things up in silvery paper and we say, "I want you to know that you matter to me." Exhausting, yes. But when it's done right, when you keep in mind the overarching message of it all, the holidays can be about something significant. They ask you to take the time out of your hectic life to celebrate those around you.

ENJOY!

—Jonathan King, Jim Stott,
and Kathy Gunst

CHAPTER

SALADS, SOUPS & APPETIZERS

WINTER RADICCHIO SLAW

SERVES 8

Here's a slaw made for winter, with Italian radicchio, fresh fennel, endive, and tart sweet apple, all tossed with a light, ginger-enhanced vinaigrette. This is not a salad that can be made hours ahead of time, though. You can, however, prepare the vinaigrette and cut all the vegetables and toss them together just before serving. This slaw goes really well with the Simplest Pork Roast (page 74) or any roasted poultry. It's delicious piled onto a leftover sandwich.

INGREDIENTS

THE VINAIGRETTE

3 tablespoons freshly squeezed lemon juice

2 teaspoons Dijon mustard

2 teaspoons finely chopped or grated fresh ginger

Salt

Freshly ground black pepper

3 tablespoons extra-virgin olive oil

: : : : :

2 heads radicchio (about 1 pound total), cored and very thinly sliced

1 medium fennel bulb (about 8 ounces), cored and very thinly sliced

2 heads endive (about 8 ounces total), cored and very thinly sliced

1 red or green tart apple, such as Granny Smith or Macoun, cut into ¼-inch sticks

¼ cup chopped scallions (green and white parts)

1. *Make the vinaigrette:* Whisk the lemon juice, mustard, and ginger together in a small bowl, and season with salt and pepper to taste. Add the oil in a slow, steady stream while whisking, and whisk until emulsified. Season to taste as needed, and set aside.

2. Place the slaw ingredients in a large bowl. Just before serving, drizzle the dressing over the vegetables, and stir to coat. Serve immediately.

WEDGE SALAD WITH BLUE CHEESE, BACON, AND ROASTED SHALLOTS

SERVES 6

Why did iceberg go out of style? When you're in the mood for something refreshing and crunchy, iceberg is so the answer. In this salad, wedges of iceberg lettuce are topped with crumbled blue cheese, bacon, and buttery roasted shallots. We pour a thick blue cheese dressing on top. Serve as a first course or with any holiday meal.

This chunky blue cheese dressing is excellent served with any mixed greens or it can be served as a dip with celery and endive spears.

INGREDIENTS

THE BLUE CHEESE DRESSING

4 ounces blue cheese, like Gorgonzola, crumbled

⅔ cup extra-virgin olive oil

¼ cup white wine vinegar

¼ cup whole milk

Salt

Freshly ground black pepper

: : : : :

2 large shallots or 4 small ones, peeled and thinly sliced

1 tablespoon olive oil

Salt

Freshly ground black pepper

4 ounces bacon (about 6 slices)

1 large head iceberg lettuce (about 1 pound)

1 ounce blue cheese, like Gorgonzola, crumbled

1. *Make the dressing:* In the container of a blender or food processor, whirl 3 ounces of the blue cheese with the oil, vinegar, milk, and salt and pepper to taste until smooth. Remove to a bowl and stir in the remaining 1 ounce of blue cheese. Taste for seasoning.

2. Place a rack in the middle of the oven and preheat to 350 degrees F.

3. Place the shallots in a small, ovenproof skillet or ramekin and toss with the oil, plus salt and pepper to taste. Roast for about 10 minutes, or until golden brown and buttery looking. Remove and let cool.

4. Cook the bacon in a large skillet about 4 to 6 minutes on each side, depending on the thickness, until crisp on both sides. Drain on paper towels. Chop into ½-inch pieces. The salad can be made ahead of time up to this point; cover and refrigerate the shallots, bacon, and dressing.

5. Remove the outside leaves of the lettuce until you get to the firm, paler leaves. Cut the whole head of lettuce in half vertically and then cut each half into 3 pieces, leaving you with 6 wedges.

6. Arrange the lettuce wedges on 6 salad plates or 1 large serving platter. Spoon a heaping tablespoon of the dressing into the center of each lettuce wedge (letting it spill down the sides). Sprinkle each wedge with some of the bacon, roasted shallots, and the 1 ounce of crumbled blue cheese. Top with a grinding of pepper and serve the remaining blue cheese dressing on the side.

ROASTED ACORN SQUASH AND BEET SALAD WITH MAPLE-RAISIN VINAIGRETTE

SERVES 6

We roast thin slices of squash until tender, then glaze them with maple syrup. Next we roast tiny red and yellow beets until tender and toss them with mixed greens and a simple maple syrup–lemon-raisin vinaigrette. Best of all, almost all the elements of this salad can be made ahead of time and assembled just before serving. This salad makes an elegant first course for any holiday meal. For an extra touch of elegance, you can drizzle the salad or the surrounding salad plates with a few drops of the Balsamic Glaze.

INGREDIENTS

THE VINAIGRETTE

¼ cup freshly squeezed lemon juice

¼ cup maple syrup

1 teaspoon Dijon mustard

⅓ cup plus 1 tablespoon olive oil

Salt

Freshly ground black pepper

⅓ cup raisins or currants

: : : : :

8 ounces yellow beets, preferably no bigger than 3 inches

8 ounces red or Chioggia beets, preferably no bigger than 3 inches

1 acorn squash (around 1 pound), peeled, seeded, and cut into ½-inch half moons

1 tablespoon olive oil

Salt

Freshly ground black pepper

⅓ cup maple syrup

8 ounces mixed greens or herb salad

Balsamic Glaze (see page 21; optional)

1. *Make the vinaigrette:* In a small bowl, whisk the lemon juice, maple syrup, and mustard together. Add the oil and whisk until smooth. Season with salt and pepper to taste. Cover and refrigerate overnight if needed. Do not add the raisins if making the vinaigrette ahead of time.

2. Place a rack in the middle of the oven and preheat to 400 degrees F.

3. Tightly wrap the beets into two aluminum foil bundles.

Continued...

...continued

Roast for 45 minutes to 1 hour, or until tender in the center when tested with a small sharp knife. Remove from the oven and let cool slightly. Peel the beets and set aside; they can be covered and refrigerated overnight.

4. Place the squash slices on a rimmed baking sheet. Toss with the oil, and salt and pepper to taste. Roast for 15 minutes. Remove and drizzle the maple syrup over the squash. Roast another 10 minutes, or until tender. Let cool. The squash can be covered and refrigerated overnight.

5. Place the salad greens in the middle of a large plate. Arrange the squash slices around the edge of the plate. Place the beets in small piles between the squash and the lettuce. Add the currants to the vinaigrette and pour half of it over the salad. Serve the remaining vinaigrette on the side. Drizzle with Balsamic Glaze, if desired.

VARIATIONS:
Scatter with Curried Maple Pecans (page 49).

Use dried cranberries instead of raisins.

Sprinkle with ½ cup crumbled blue cheese or goat cheese.

Add ¼ cup minced fresh chives to the vinaigrette.

THE MAGIC OF BALSAMIC GLAZE

This is one of those recipes that leaves them guessing. If you simmer a few cups of balsamic vinegar over low heat and watch it like a hawk, you will be rewarded with a gorgeous, jet-black, syrupy-sweet glaze. That's the recipe. Let's go over it, again: Take 2 cups balsamic vinegar (it need not be the super-fancy expensive kind) and place it in a medium saucepan. Simmer over low heat for 40 minutes to an hour. You'll know it's done when it coats the back of a spoon and is thick and syrupy. Remove from the heat. Let cool. Place in a bottle (one of those plastic bottles with the squeeze top that they use for serving ketchup and mustard in diners) or a small, glass jar. Seal and refrigerate. The glaze will last for several weeks. Bring it to room temperature before using for a good, pourable consistency.

What do you do with it? Balsamic glaze adds a sweet, tart, syrupy flavor to almost everything. Drizzle a few drops on soups and stews; add it to vinaigrettes; garnish a salad, meat, poultry, or vegetable dish; pour it into a sauté pan to deglaze chicken, fish, or meat dishes; drizzle over sandwiches, cheese, or ice cream, fresh figs, strawberries, apples, and pears. Experiment.

F.Y.I.: Balsamic glaze makes a wonderful holiday gift. Package it in a small glass mason jar, and add a handmade note about all the possible uses!!

WINTER SPINACH SALAD WITH ROASTED PEARS, BLUE CHEESE TOASTS, AND DRIED CRANBERRY VINAIGRETTE

SERVES 8

Although there are several elements in this salad, everything can be prepared ahead of time and assembled at the last minute, making this an ideal holiday dish. We love the winter flavors found in this salad—the tender green of the spinach leaves, the chewy red dried cranberries, and the buttery pale pears. The blue cheese toasts are so good you'll want a few extra to snack on.

INGREDIENTS

1 teaspoon unsalted butter

2 firm-ripe d'Anjou pears (see Notes)

1½ teaspoons sugar

:::::

DRIED CRANBERRY VINAIGRETTE

½ cup dried cranberries

⅓ cup cider vinegar

2 tablespoons pomegranate molasses, maple syrup, or honey (see Notes)

1 tablespoon Dijon mustard

Salt

Freshly ground black pepper

⅓ cup extra-virgin olive oil

:::::

½ cup (1½ ounces) sliced almonds

½ cup dried cranberries

:::::

BLUE CHEESE TOASTS

Eight ½-inch slices ciabatta or crusty French or Italian bread

Extra-virgin olive oil for brushing

5 to 6 ounces blue cheese, such as Gorgonzola or bleu d'Auvergne, thinly sliced

:::::

6 ounces baby spinach

1. Place a rack in the middle of the oven and preheat to 450 degrees F.

2. Grease a small baking sheet with the butter. Peel and core the pears and cut each into 8 wedges. Toss the pears and sugar together in a bowl and place on the buttered baking sheet, cut-sides down. Roast for 15 to 20 minutes, or until soft and browned on the undersides. Transfer pears to a piece of waxed paper and let cool completely. The pears can be made up to 4 hours ahead.

Continued...

. . . continued

3. *Meanwhile, make the vinaigrette:* In a blender, whirl the ½ cup cranberries, vinegar, molasses, and mustard until smooth and uniformly pink. Season with salt and pepper to taste. With the machine running, add the ⅓ cup oil in a slow, steady stream, and blend until smooth. Season again with salt and pepper, if necessary. Set aside.

4. Toast the almonds on a baking sheet for 3 to 5 minutes, or until lightly browned. Transfer to a small bowl to cool, then stir in the second ½ cup cranberries.

5. *Make the blue cheese toasts:* Reduce the oven temperature to 400 degrees F. Cut each slice of bread in half, so you have 16 halves. Brush both sides of each piece with some of the oil, and toast on a baking sheet for 3 to 4 minutes per side, until lightly browned. Remove from the oven, and divide the blue cheese between the toasts, crumbling the cheese up a little as you go. (The toasts can be made ahead up to this point and refrigerated, up to 4 hours.) Return the toasts to the oven and bake for 4 to 5 minutes, until the blue cheese has melted.

6. Place the spinach in a large bowl, add half the almond/cranberry mixture, add the vinaigrette to taste, and mix well. Arrange the dressed greens on a platter or on individual salad plates, and garnish with additional nuts and berries, roasted pears, and blue cheese toasts. Serve immediately.

NOTES:
Look for pears that are just beginning to get soft, but are still somewhat firm.

Pomegranate molasses is a thick, dark syrup used in Mediterranean cooking. It can be found in specialty food shops, or the gourmet section of many supermarkets.

VARIATIONS:
Peel and core a tart apple instead of the pear.

Substitute goat cheese or a hard grating cheese, like Parmesan, for the blue cheese.

Substitute dried cherries for the cranberries.

Substitute coarsely chopped walnuts, pecans, pistachios, or your favorite nuts for the almonds.

WATERCRESS, TANGERINE, AND FENNEL SALAD WITH SPICE-ENCRUSTED TUNA

SERVES 8

This winter salad makes an ideal first course for a holiday or a light main-course dinner salad (a refreshing change from all the rich foods of the season). All the elements can be prepared ahead of time and assembled just before serving. Look for really fresh sushi-grade tuna.

INGREDIENTS

THE DRESSING

⅔ cup freshly squeezed tangerine or orange juice

⅓ cup plus 1 tablespoon olive oil

Sea salt

Freshly ground black pepper

∷∷∷

2 tablespoons fennel seeds

2 tablespoons coriander seeds

⅛ teaspoon sea salt

Generous grinding coarsely ground black pepper

1 pound *very fresh* tuna, such as yellowfin or ahi

4 ounces watercress, stems removed unless they are very small and tender

1 medium fennel bulb, fronds removed, cored and very thinly sliced

1½ tablespoons canola oil

2 tangerines, peeled and separated into sections, with each section cut in half

1. *Make the dressing:* In a small bowl, whisk together the juice, oil, and salt and pepper to taste.

2. Place the fennel and coriander seeds in a coffee grinder or small spice grinder and pulse until coarsely ground; you don't want them finely ground or powdery. Remove to a small bowl and mix in the salt and pepper. Coat the tuna in the spice mixture on all sides, pressing it on to adhere well.

Continued...

... *continued*

3. Arrange the watercress and fennel in the center of a large serving plate or divide and place in the middle of 8 small salad plates.

4. In a large skillet, heat the oil over medium-high heat. When the oil is hot (almost smoking), add the tuna. Let cook 2 to 3 minutes on each side; 2 minutes will give you a well-seared surface with a very rare center. If you prefer your tuna less rare, cook it another minute or two. We like it rare inside so that when you cut into it there's a well-seared layer next to a gorgeous almost-rare center.

5. Let cool for 1 minute; carve the tuna into ½-inch slices. Place them in overlapping layers down the middle of the plate(s) and surround with the tangerine sections. Just before serving, drizzle a little dressing over the tuna and serve the remaining dressing on the side.

VARIATIONS:

Substitute a thick salmon steak for the tuna and cook about 3 to 4 minutes on each side, or until almost cooked through.

Use orange sections or blood oranges instead of the tangerines.

BUTTERNUT SQUASH SOUP WITH CURRIED PECANS, APPLE, AND GOAT CHEESE

SERVES 6

This is a soothing, comforting soup to take you through the crazy rush of the holidays. You can make it in large batches, and freeze or refrigerate it for several days. The curried pecans will keep for several days as well. We love a big bowl of this bright orange soup with a salad and crusty bread for a simple midweek meal.

INGREDIENTS

THE SOUP

1½ tablespoons canola oil

2 medium onions, finely chopped

Salt

Freshly ground black pepper

3 pounds butternut squash, peeled and cut into 1-inch cubes

4 cups chicken or vegetable broth

:::::

1 cup Curried Maple Pecans (page 49), chopped

4 ounces goat cheese, crumbled

1 tart apple, like Pink Lady, finely chopped

12 whole sage leaves

1. *Make the soup:* In a large pot, heat the oil over low heat. Add the onions, plus salt and pepper to taste, and cook, stirring frequently, for 12 minutes, or until the onions are golden brown and caramelized. Add the squash and cook 5 minutes, stirring well. Raise the heat to high, add the broth, and bring to a boil. Reduce the heat to low and let it simmer, covered, for about 15 minutes, or until the squash is tender when tested with a small, sharp knife. Let cool slightly.

2. Working in batches, puree the soup in the container of a food processor or blender. Return the soup to the pot and keep warm over low heat. (The soup can be made a day ahead of time, covered and refrigerated, or frozen for up to 3 months.)

3. Place the hot soup in serving bowls and top with some of the chopped pecans, goat cheese, apple, and sage leaves. Serve any remaining pecans, cheese, or apples on the side.

VARIATIONS:

Add chopped ripe pear instead of apple.

Add 1 to 2 tablespoons chopped fresh cilantro to the soup with the broth and sprinkle another tablespoon on top just before serving.

Sauté the apple slices in 1 tablespoon butter for 1 to 2 minutes on each side, or until just turning golden brown.

LOBSTER STEW WITH SAFFRON CREAM

MAKES 4 TO 6 SMALL PORTIONS

Don't be scared off by the idea of saffron. It's an earthy, exotic spice (one of the world's most prized), and a little bit goes a long way. Look for saffron in specialty food shops or in the spice section of good food stores, and try sprinkling it into soups, stews, and rice dishes (it's the distinguishing flavor of the classic Spanish dish paella).

Because this stew is so rich and satisfying, we like to serve it in very small portions—in a small bowl, or a demitasse or espresso cup with a tiny espresso spoon. The Saffron Cream needs to chill for several hours or overnight. If you're serving a crowd the recipe can easily be doubled or even tripled.

INGREDIENTS

THE SAFFRON CREAM	THE LOBSTER STEW
1 cup heavy cream	1 tablespoon unsalted butter
1 teaspoon crumbled saffron (see Note)	2 shallots, finely chopped
	Salt
	Freshly ground black pepper
	1 cup whole milk
	⅓ cup heavy cream
	1 pound cooked lobster meat, from about two 2-pound lobsters

1. *Make the Saffron Cream:* In a medium saucepan, heat the cream over low heat until just simmering. Crumble in the saffron, crushing it between your fingers, and stir into the hot cream to blend thoroughly. Cover and refrigerate for several hours, or overnight.

2. *Make the stew:* In a medium saucepan, melt the butter over low heat. Add the shallots, plus salt and pepper to taste, and cook, stirring

Continued...

...*continued*

occasionally, for about 6 minutes, or until the shallots are softened and a pale golden color. In a separate pan, heat the milk and cream together over low heat.

3. Meanwhile, pour the cooled Saffron Cream into a mixing bowl and, using an electric beater or a whisk, whip until soft peaks form.

4. Cut three quarters of the lobster into ½-inch chunks. Finely chop the remaining lobster meat. Add all of the lobster to the shallots and cook 1 minute. Pour the warm milk/cream on top and let cook about 3 minutes on low heat, or until heated through.

5. Serve the lobster stew in small bowls or demitasse cups. Spoon a dollop of Saffron Cream on top of each and serve hot.

NOTE:
You can substitute good Hungarian sweet paprika for the saffron, but you won't get the same deliciously earthy flavor and the color of the cream won't be as beautiful or intense.

VARIATIONS:
Substitute 1 pound fresh sea scallops for the lobster. Cut the scallops in half (or in quarters if they are very large) and cook with the shallots for 3 minutes before adding the hot milk mixture.

Substitute a dozen raw, shucked oysters or clams for the lobster, making sure to add any accumulated oyster or clam juice along with the milk/cream mixture.

OYSTERS BAKED ON CREAMED SPINACH WITH PARMESAN-PANKO CRUST

SERVES 4 TO 6

If you want to serve one dish for the holidays that will keep them talking, this is the one to try. It is our take on the classic New Orleans dish Oysters Rockefeller. We bake freshly shucked oysters on top of creamy garlic-laced spinach and top them off with a mixture of Parmesan cheese and panko breadcrumbs. The creamy spinach layer topped with the soft briny oysters and then the crunchy topping is a perfect balance of flavors and textures. The oysters make a great first course, hors d'oeuvre, or dinner.

Make the spinach mixture ahead of time, have your topping ready, and then ask friends to help you shuck the oysters just before serving. You can also ask your fishmonger to shuck the oysters for you (be sure it's the same day you're serving them), but be sure to keep the shells.

INGREDIENTS

1 tablespoon olive oil

2 teaspoons minced garlic

8 ounces baby spinach

Salt

Freshly ground black pepper

¼ cup heavy cream

½ cup panko breadcrumbs

3 tablespoons grated Parmesan cheese

2 to 3 cups kosher salt

12 large oysters, shucked, lower (deeply curved) shells reserved

1½ teaspoons unsalted butter, cut into 12 pieces

1. Heat a large, heavy skillet over medium heat. When hot, add the oil, then the garlic, and stir for 10 seconds. Add the spinach a handful at a time, stirring and adding more as it wilts in the pan. When all the spinach has been added, season with salt and pepper to taste. Cook for a few minutes, stirring

Continued...

…continued

constantly, until all the spinach is wilted. Add the cream and simmer 5 to 7 minutes, stirring frequently, until the cream has been absorbed and reduced almost entirely. Set the pan aside to cool. (If making the day before, transfer the spinach to an airtight container and refrigerate overnight.)

2. Stir the breadcrumbs and Parmesan together in a small bowl. Season with salt and pepper, and set aside (or refrigerate overnight).

3. Preheat the broiler on high heat. Fill a rimmed baking sheet with a layer of kosher salt about ½ inch deep and arrange the baking sheet about 3 inches from the heating element. Nestle the curved part of the oyster shells into the salt. Divide the spinach mixture between the 12 shells. Top each pile of spinach with a raw oyster, then sprinkle each oyster with a tablespoon of the breadcrumb mixture. Dot each oyster with a tiny piece of butter, and broil for about 3 minutes, rotating the pan if necessary, or until the breadcrumbs are evenly browned, the oysters are cooked, and the spinach is warmed through. Serve immediately.

VARIATIONS:
Substitute sea scallops for the oysters. Use scallop shells (available in fish shops) and broil about 4 minutes, depending on the size of the scallops, or until just cooked through.

Substitute raw clams for the oysters and broil for 2 to 3 minutes.

HOPE'S SMOKED SALMON CRACKERS WITH RED ONION–CAPER SAUCE

MAKES ABOUT 40 APPETIZERS; SERVES ABOUT 12 TO 15

Kathy's friend Hope Murphy introduced her to this simple appetizer years ago and it became an instant hit. Just spread spicy wasabi crackers (available in most grocery stores) with cream cheese, thin slices of smoked salmon, and a red onion–caper sauce to make an elegant hors d'oeuvre. Make the sauce an hour ahead of time and assemble the crackers just before serving. The recipe can easily be doubled or tripled to feed a large crowd.

INGREDIENTS

1 medium red onion, diced

¼ cup capers, drained

¼ cup olive oil

2 tablespoons red wine vinegar

½ teaspoon Worcestershire sauce

6 ounces cream cheese, at room temperature

One 3½-ounce package Ka-Me Rice Crunch Wasabi crackers or any thin cracker, preferably a spicy variety

4 ounces smoked salmon, cut into 1-inch pieces

1. In a small bowl, mix together the onion, capers, oil, vinegar, and Worcestershire sauce and let sit, covered and refrigerated, for an hour.

2. Spread the cream cheese on the crackers and top each one with a piece of the salmon. Top each with a generous teaspoon of the sauce and serve immediately.

VARIATIONS:

Use soft goat cheese instead of cream cheese.

Add ¼ cup minced chives or finely chopped scallions sprinkled on top of the final dish.

Add ¼ cup finely chopped pitted olives (black and/or green) to the onion/caper sauce.

Substitute smoked trout for the salmon.

TARRAGON CRAB CANAPÉS

MAKES 8 CANAPÉS; SERVES 4

Small rounds of toasted white bread create an easy base for these savory canapés. Make the toasts and crabmeat mixture ahead of time and assemble just before serving.

INGREDIENTS

2 tablespoons unsalted butter

4 slices white bread

2 tablespoons mayonnaise

1 tablespoon freshly squeezed lemon juice

1 tablespoon chopped fresh tarragon, plus more for garnish

2 teaspoons lemon zest

Salt

Freshly ground black pepper

8 ounces fresh lump crabmeat

1. Place a rack in the middle of the oven and preheat to 425 degrees F.

2. Melt the butter in a small saucepan over low heat.

3. Using the top of a juice glass or a small biscuit cutter, cut two (2½-inch) rounds out of each slice of bread. Brush the rounds on both sides with the butter, and place on a baking sheet. Bake for about 2 minutes per side, or until lightly browned. Set the toasts aside to cool. (Toasts can be made ahead and cooled, then stored in an airtight container overnight.)

4. Stir the mayonnaise, lemon juice, chopped tarragon, and lemon zest together in a bowl, and season with salt and pepper to taste. Stir in the crabmeat, then season to taste with additional salt and pepper, if necessary.

5. Pile about 1 tablespoon of salad onto each toast, and serve.

VARIATIONS:

Substitute 8 ounces cooked lobster meat, chopped into ½-inch pieces, for the crabmeat.

Substitute fresh chives or finely chopped scallions for the tarragon.

Substitute lime zest and juice for the lemon.

Place the finished canapés on the side of a tossed salad, or on top of a bed of lightly dressed arugula and watercress.

MINI LOBSTER CUPS

SERVES 4 TO 7

Mini phyllo (or filo) shells—available in the freezer section of your supermarket—are perfect for getting through the holiday season. Here we bake them and fill them with a simple lobster–cream cheese and chive mixture. They make an ideal first course, or served on top of mixed greens.

INGREDIENTS

15 frozen mini phyllo shells

4 ounces cream cheese, at room temperature

¼ pound cooked lobster meat, coarsely chopped

1 teaspoon grated lemon zest

1 tablespoon minced fresh chives, plus a few chive sprigs for garnish

Pinch cayenne

1. Place a rack in the middle of the oven and preheat to 350 degrees F. Arrange the phyllo shells on a baking sheet and bake about 10 minutes, or until the shells are warm.

2. Meanwhile, in a bowl, mix the cream cheese until smooth. Gently fold in all the lobster *except* 2 tablespoons. Fold in the lemon zest, minced chives, and cayenne.

3. Remove the shells from the oven and let cool a minute.

Divide the cream cheese/lobster mixture between the shells. Divide the remaining 2 tablespoons lobster on top of the cups and garnish with the chive sprigs before serving.

VARIATIONS:
Substitute crabmeat for the lobster.

Add 1 teaspoon chopped fresh tarragon to the lobster mixture.

Top the finished cup with a teaspoon of red or black caviar for an elegant presentation.

INSTANT HOLIDAY APPETIZERS FROM THE PANTRY

The doorbell rings and it's your neighbors dropping off a gift. Old friends are in town for the holidays and would love to "just stop by." You just bumped into your son's favorite soccer coach in the store and, without thinking, said, "Why don't you come by for a drink?"

The truth is: You have very little food in the refrigerator and no time to plan or start cooking anything elaborate. Here are some really simple appetizers, made primarily from foods found in a well-stocked pantry or refrigerator. The staple to keep on hand is in bold:

* Drain a **can of beans** (white cannellini beans are particularly good) and rinse well. Place them in a food processor or blender with a few tablespoons of **olive oil**, a clove of **garlic**, and some **herbs** and whirl until smooth, and you've got an instant bean dip. Serve with **crackers** or warm **pita bread** cut into triangles.

* Serve **jarred salsa** with raw or steamed vegetables, **crackers**, and a variety of **chips**. Or place a tablespoon of salsa on each tortilla chip and top with a dollop of **sour cream** mixed with a dash of hot pepper sauce.

* Hard boil a few **eggs**; cool and peel. Cut in half and scoop out the yolks and place in a bowl. Mash with a tablespoon or two of **mayonnaise** and 1 to 2 tablespoons **black or green olive tapenade**. Place the filling back in the egg whites and serve.

* Mix 2 cups **cream cheese** (at room temperature) with chopped **herbs** (fresh or dried). Spread on **crackers or pita chips** and top with **smoked salmon or trout** and paper-thin slices of **lemon**.

* Serve a **store-bought pâté** with **mango chutney**, a bottle of **French pickles (cornichons)**, **French mustard**, and crisp **crackers**.

* Surround a small log of **goat cheese** in a small roasting pan with a cup of slightly drained, coarsely chopped, **jarred sun-dried tomatoes** and a handful of **pine nuts** (or your favorite nut) and bake at 350 degrees F for about 15 minutes, or until the cheese begins to soften and almost melt. Serve with **crackers** or slices of **bread.**

* Mash **blue cheese** with a fork and add sour cream and a touch of **mustard** and serve in endive spears, celery, or on **crackers or flatbread.**

* Mix 1 cup **sour cream** with ⅓ cup **jarred olive tapenade**, a squirt of **lemon juice**, and 1 teaspoon of **olive oil** for an instant olive dip. Serve with warm **pita bread, crackers, chips,** or strips of peppers and other raw or lightly steamed vegetables.

* Open a jar of **roasted red peppers** and a **can of anchovies.** Lay the pepper strips on a large plate and crisscross 2 anchovies over each pepper in an "X" shape, then drizzle with **olive oil** and **balsamic vinegar**. You can also sprinkle them with a few tablespoons of drained capers. Serve with crusty **bread or crackers.**

* Drain a **can of tuna** and chop loosely with a fork. Mix with a drizzle of **olive oil**, a tablespoon or so of drained **capers,** and **lemon juice.** Serve with **crackers,** vegetables, etc.

* Mix 1 cup **cream cheese** (at room temperature) with freshly ground pepper, 1 tablespoon **lemon juice,** and chopped **chives.** Place a piece of **smoked salmon** on a work surface and add a tablespoon of the cream cheese mixture. Roll into a fat cigar shape. Cut into bite-sized pieces.

INDIAN-SPICED MEATBALLS WITH YOGURT AND MANGO CHUTNEY

MAKES 25 ONE-INCH MEATBALLS; SERVES 6 TO 8 AS AN APPETIZER

Around the holidays we tend to make traditional favorites with comforting, tried and true flavors. Here we step outside the box a bit and mix ground beef, pork, and veal with pungent Indian flavors—fennel and mustard seeds, ginger, chile flakes, and fresh cilantro—and form the mixture into tiny, bite-sized meatballs. The meatballs are then dipped into thick, Greek-style yogurt and chutney. They make a wonderful hors d'oeuvre or can be served as a first course on top of spicy greens—watercress and arugula—with warm pita bread or crisp Indian bread (*naan*).

The meatballs can be made several hours ahead of time and reheated just before serving.

INGREDIENTS

THE MEATBALLS

About 3 tablespoons canola or peanut oil

1 tablespoon black or yellow mustard seeds

1 tablespoon fennel seeds

Pinch red chile flakes

1½ tablespoons minced fresh ginger

3 tablespoons minced scallions (white and green parts)

Salt

Freshly ground black pepper

6 ounces ground beef

5 ounces ground pork

5 ounces ground veal

1 large egg

⅔ cup plus 1 tablespoon panko or regular dried breadcrumbs

¼ cup Greek-style plain yogurt

2 ½ tablespoons minced fresh cilantro

¼ cup white sesame seeds

: : : : :

1 ½ cups Greek-style plain yogurt

1 ½ cups mango or other chutney

Continued...

…*continued*

1. *Make the meatballs:* In a small skillet, heat 1 tablespoon of the oil over low heat. Add the mustard and fennel seeds and cook 2 minutes, stirring once or twice. Add the chile flakes, ginger, 1 tablespoon of the scallions, and salt and pepper to taste, and cook for about 2 minutes, stirring, until the seeds begin to pop and the ginger smells fragrant, being careful not to let the mixture burn. Remove from the heat and let cool.

2. In a large bowl, mix together the beef, pork, veal, and egg until thoroughly incorporated. Season with salt and pepper to taste. Add the cooled spice mixture and the oil from the skillet. Mix well. Add ⅓ cup plus 1 tablespoon breadcrumbs, the ¼ cup yogurt, the remaining 2 tablespoons of scallions, and cilantro and mix well. The mixture should be moist but hold together. (You can make the mixture several hours ahead of time; cover and refrigerate until ready to cook.)

3. Place the remaining ⅓ cup breadcrumbs on a large plate or bowl and mix in the sesame seeds, and salt and pepper to taste.

4. Use a tablespoon measure to form 25 small, rounded meatballs. Lightly coat the meatballs in the breadcrumb–sesame seed mixture, pressing the mixture onto the meatballs lightly.

5. In a large, heavy skillet, heat the remaining 2 tablespoons of oil over medium-low heat. When the oil is hot (add a touch of breadcrumb to the skillet; the oil should immediately sizzle, but not burn), add several meatballs, making sure not to crowd the skillet. Cook 8 to 10 minutes (about 4 minutes per side), or until the meatballs are golden brown and cooked through (cut open one to make sure there is no sign of pinkness). Place several layers of paper towel on a baking sheet and drain the meatballs thoroughly. Cook the remaining meatballs, adding more oil if needed.

6. The meatballs should be served hot after draining for 30 seconds or they can be made several hours ahead of time. Cover and refrigerate until ready to cook. To reheat: Place the meatballs on a baking sheet in a preheated 350 degree F oven for about 5 minutes, or until hot.

7. Serve the hot meatballs with bowls of the yogurt and chutney.

CURRIED MAPLE PECANS

MAKES 1 CUP

We like to serve these sweet and slightly spicy nuts with cocktails, cheese platters, sprinkled over salads, and in Butternut Squash Soup with Curried Pecans, Apples, and Goat Cheese (page 28). Make a double or triple batch to have some on hand for last-minute entertaining, or to bring as a house gift (see page 117).

INGREDIENTS

1 tablespoon unsalted butter

½ teaspoon curry powder

½ teaspoon ground ginger

⅛ teaspoon salt

Generous grinding freshly ground black pepper

1 cup (3 ½ ounces) pecan halves

¼ cup maple syrup

1. In a large, heavy skillet, melt the butter over low heat. Add the curry, ginger, salt, and pepper, stirring well to mix the spices into the butter. Let cook 2 minutes.

2. Add the pecans and cook another 2 minutes. Pour the maple syrup on top and, stirring frequently, cook another 2 to 3 minutes, or until the syrup has thickened a bit and the nuts look glazed.

3. Pour the nuts onto waxed or parchment paper or foil, being careful to separate them, as they tend to clump together.

When cool, move the nuts to a well-sealed container in a cool spot.

VARIATIONS:

Try this recipe using a mixture of nuts: walnuts, almonds, pistachios, Brazil nuts, etc.

Add a dash of cayenne pepper along with the curry and ginger for a slightly spicy bite.

Substitute a flowery honey, such as orange blossom, for the maple syrup.

Add ⅛ teaspoon ground cumin with the curry and ginger.

MAIN
COURSES

BEEF TENDERLOIN WITH HORSERADISH CRUST, ROASTED POTATOES, AND GARLIC

SERVES 8

The holidays are the perfect time to splurge on beef tenderloin. Good beef tenderloin can cost a small fortune, but keep in mind that this is a cut that's pure meat—no fat, bones, or excess. This dish is simple as can be, but also very elegant. Ask your butcher for the best center-cut tenderloin.

You can sear the meat and prepare the crust and then cover and refrigerate the meat until you're ready to roast. Be sure to take the meat out of the refrigerator 15 to 20 minutes before roasting to bring it to room temperature.

INGREDIENTS

About 20 new (baby) potatoes, white and red, or any assortment

4 tablespoons olive oil

1 tablespoon chopped fresh rosemary or 1 teaspoon dried

Salt

Freshly ground black pepper

One 5-ounce bottle white horseradish

One 3½-pound center-cut beef tenderloin, tied with butcher string

1 tablespoon minced fresh thyme or 1 teaspoon dried

2 tablespoons Dijon mustard

2 heads garlic, ¼ inch cut off the top to just expose the cloves

1. Place a rack in the middle of the oven and preheat to 400 degrees F.

2. Place the potatoes in a large roasting pan and toss with 1 tablespoon of the oil, the rosemary, and salt and pepper to taste. Roast for 30 minutes, tossing them once or twice, or until beginning to brown, but not cooked through. Remove and set aside.

Continued...

...*continued*

3. While the potatoes are roasting, place the horseradish in a fine-mesh strainer and drain off any liquid.

4. Season the beef on all sides with salt and pepper and the thyme.

5. In a large skillet, heat 2 tablespoons of the oil over high heat. Sear the meat on all sides, about 2 minutes per side, reducing the heat if the meat starts to burn. Remove from the heat and let cool thoroughly. (The meat and potatoes can be prepared several hours ahead of time up to this point. Cover and refrigerate until ready to roast.

Be sure to remove the meat 15 to 20 minutes before roasting to bring the meat to room temperature.)

6. Preheat the oven to 425 degrees F. Place the meat on a roasting rack inside the roasting pan. The potatoes can either go underneath the beef (they will be basted with the beef juices) or you can push them off to the sides. Pat the mustard on top of the tenderloin, and then top with the drained horseradish, pressing down to form a crust. Season with salt and pepper. Drizzle the remaining tablespoon of oil on top of the horseradish crust. Place the garlic next to the potatoes.

7. Roast the beef and potatoes on the middle shelf for 45 minutes to 1 hour, or until the internal temperature of the meat is 140 degrees F for medium-rare. (The temperature will continue to rise once you take the meat out of the oven.) Let sit for 5 minutes, loosely covered with foil, before carving. The garlic can be served whole or squeezed out of the skins and served alongside the meat and potatoes.

STANDING RIB ROAST STUDDED WITH GARLIC

SERVES 12 TO 14

There are a few things that make the difference between a good standing rib roast and a great one. First is the beef. This is the holiday season, so you should go all out and visit the finest butcher in the area; ask for top-quality (preferably organic or naturally raised) prime beef. Ask your butcher to cut out the chine bone to make carving easier. Figure on at least half a pound per person— leftovers are highly desirable.

The next "trick" is the temperature. We like to roast the beef at a high beginning temperature (around 450 degrees F) and then lower it once the meat is seared and roast at 325 degrees for the remainder of the time. The result is meat with a gorgeous brown crust and medium-rare, tender, juicy meat inside. We also love surrounding the roasting meat with small onions, whole heads of garlic, and small potatoes. The Sharp Cheddar and Herb Popovers (page 107) and several of the vegetable purees (pages 86, 87, and 89) would make this a fabulous holiday meal. Don't forget an extraordinary, full-bodied red wine.

INGREDIENTS

One well-aged 15- to 18-pound standing rib roast (about 7 ribs), chine bone removed, trimmed of excess fat and tied

Sea salt

Freshly ground black pepper

6 cloves garlic, peeled and very thinly sliced

36 small boiling or cipollini onions, peeled and left whole

36 new (baby) potatoes, left whole, or 12 larger potatoes, peeled and quartered

4 heads garlic, ¼ inch cut off the top to just expose the cloves

¼ cup minced fresh thyme

1. Place a rack in the middle of the oven and preheat to 450 degrees F.

2. Season the beef liberally all over with salt and pepper. Using a small, sharp knife, make several small slits in the fat along the top of the beef and gently insert the garlic

Continued...

...*continued*

slices. Place the beef fat-side up on a roasting rack in a large roasting pan. Roast the beef for 20 minutes.

3. Place the onions, potatoes, and garlic in a bowl and toss with salt, pepper, and the thyme.

4. Reduce the oven temperature to 325 degrees F and continue roasting for 2 hours. Arrange the vegetables around the beef, in the bottom of the roasting pan. Roast for another 1½ to 2 hours, until the internal temperature of the meat reaches 140 degrees F for medium-rare. Stir the vegetables well to coat with any juices collected on the bottom of the roasting pan and baste the beef and the vegetables once or twice during the final hour of roasting so they brown evenly.

5. Remove from the oven and place on a carving board or wooden board; cover loosely with foil for 15 minutes before carving to let the meat juices settle. Remove the excess fat from the pan juices by tipping the roasting pan to the side and spooning off the fat that rises to the top.

6. *Carve the beef.* You can serve everyone a whole rib or slice the meat off the ribs for a smaller portion. Serve with the potatoes, onions, and garlic (popped out of the skins), with the pan juices spooned on top.

ROASTING PRIMER

This is the time of year when we roast big cuts of meat—beef, pork, lamb, turkey—and many questions arise. Here are a few tips that make roasting simple:

* Always preheat the oven and arrange the racks so that your roasting pan and roast will fit without touching the walls of the oven.

* Roasts should always come out of the refrigerator at least 15 minutes before being placed in the oven to bring the meat to room temperature. If you roast a chilled piece of meat, it will throw off the cooking time.

* Make sure your roasting pan is big enough for the roast and any surrounding vegetables. A crowded pan will steam the meat and not roast properly.

HOW LONG TO ROAST?

* The internal temperature of meat will continue to rise when the roast is removed from the oven, so plan accordingly. Compensate by removing the meat when it's about 5 degrees below the desired temperature.

* When using a meat thermometer to gauge the internal temperature of a roast, always insert the thermometer in the thickest part of the meat, making sure it's not touching the bone.

* **BEEF:** 130 to 140 degrees F for rare; 145 to 160 F for medium-rare to medium; and 160 to 170 F for well-done meat with no sign of pinkness.

* **PORK:** 140 degrees F for rare or slightly pink; 150 to 160 degrees F for medium-rare to medium. Precooked ham is safe to eat when it reaches an internal temperature of 140 degrees F.

* **LAMB:** 135 degrees F for rare or pink meat; 140 to 145 degrees F for medium-rare, or slightly pink meat; 160 degrees F for medium meat, which is pink/gray; 165 to 170 degrees F for well-done meat with no sign of pinkness.

* **POULTRY:** Temperature is not always the best method to gauge whether or not a turkey or chicken is cooked. Here are a few alternate methods: Try piercing the inside of the thigh; if the juices run yellow and not pink the roast is ready. Wiggle the drumstick; if it feels loose, the bird is done. If you want to use a thermometer for a whole bird, place it into the thickest part of the breast, near the "armpit;" the internal temperature should be at least 170 degrees F. For chicken, place the thermometer in the inner thigh; the internal temperature should be at least 180 degrees F.

BRISKET WITH WINTER VEGETABLES

SERVES 6 TO 8

Chanukah—the "Festival of Lights"—is a tough holiday for many Jews. Let's face it, it's not easy competing with Christmas. But the traditional foods that are served during the eight-day festival more than make up for the lack of a decorated tree, Santa, and all those presents. Brisket is a holiday tradition for many families—a deliciously moist cut of beef that is slowly simmered for hours with root vegetables. Brisket is ideal for any winter or holiday meal because, like so many stews, it's best made a day ahead of time and reheated just before serving. Serve with horseradish and/or applesauce. The Apple Cider Jelly (page 110) is also delicious with brisket.

INGREDIENTS

About 1 cup all-purpose flour

Salt

Freshly ground black pepper

One 5- to 6-pound brisket, excess fat removed

About 2 tablespoons vegetable or canola oil

1½ tablespoons olive oil

5 yellow or red onions, quartered

2 large leeks, trimmed, cut lengthwise in half, and then into 2-inch pieces

3 cloves garlic, sliced

8 carrots, cut in half lengthwise and then into 2-inch pieces

6 celery stalks, cut into 2-inch pieces

6 medium parsnips, cut in half lengthwise and then into 2-inch pieces

1 cup finely chopped fresh parsley

2 tablespoons tomato paste

1 cup dry red wine

1 cup beef broth

1 bay leaf

1. Place the flour, salt, and pepper in a large bowl and season the brisket on both sides, shaking off any excess.

2. In a large casserole, heat 1½ tablespoons of the vegetable oil over medium-high heat until hot, about 2 minutes. Add the meat and brown on all sides, about 5 minutes. If the pan dries out, add the remaining ½ tablespoon of oil. Remove the meat and clean out the pot.

Continued...

...*continued*

3. In the same pot, heat the olive oil over low heat. Add the onions, leeks, and garlic and cook, stirring, for 5 minutes. Add the carrots, celery, parsnips, and half the parsley and cook another 5 minutes, making sure to stir the vegetables around thoroughly. Season with salt and pepper to taste. Add the meat back to the pot. Spread the tomato paste on top of the meat.

4. Raise the heat to high and add the wine and broth and bring to a boil. Reduce the heat to low, add the bay leaf, and cook, covered, for about 2 hours, spooning the sauce on top of the meat every 30 minutes or so. The meat is ready when it feels tender when gently prodded with a small, sharp knife. Taste the sauce for seasoning. Let cool 10 minutes off the heat before serving.

5. If making the brisket a day ahead of time, cover and refrigerate overnight. Spoon off any excess fat that has risen to the surface. Reheat in a 350 degree F oven for about 20 minutes, or until hot and bubbling throughout.

6. Transfer the meat to a carving board and cut into ½-inch slices. Serve the meat topped with the vegetables and juices from the pot. Sprinkle with the remaining parsley. Season to taste.

BUTTERFLIED LAMB WITH SWISS CHARD–PINE NUT–PARMESAN STUFFING

SERVES 4 TO 6

We tend to think of butterflied leg of lamb as a summer dish, but when you take leg of lamb and remove the bone there is a perfect opening for a wintry stuffing. We sauté Swiss chard (you could also use spinach or kale) with garlic, and mix it with toasted pine nuts and grated Parmesan cheese. The red and green stuffing—which comes out in a spiral shape when the meat is sliced—is perfect for any holiday dinner.

We've found that it's much easier working with half a butterflied leg of lamb than dealing with the entire leg. The roast cooks faster and is much easier to stuff and carve. This recipe is for a 3-pound boneless (half) leg of lamb, which will serve 4 to 6; so if you're feeding a crowd, we suggest ordering two boned half legs of lamb rather than one large one.

Serve the lamb with roasted potatoes, Sweet Winter Squash Gratin (page 92) or Orange-Scented Mashed Butternut Squash (page 89), the Winter Spinach Salad with Roasted Pears, Blue Cheese Toasts, and Dried Cranberry Vinaigrette (page 22), and Apple Cider Jelly (page 110).

INGREDIENTS

THE SWISS CHARD–PINE NUT–PARMESAN STUFFING

1 cup (3½ ounces) pine nuts (pignoli)

1½ tablespoons olive oil

2 cloves garlic, finely chopped

1½ pounds (1 large bunch) Swiss chard, well washed and dried, and coarsely chopped

1 large egg, lightly beaten

Salt

Freshly ground black pepper

⅓ cup grated Parmesan cheese

: : : : :

One 3-pound boneless half leg of lamb, trimmed of excess fat (see Note)

Salt

Freshly ground black pepper

1 tablespoon olive oil

1. *Make the stuffing:* Place the nuts in a small skillet over medium-low heat. Cook, stirring frequently, for about 5 minutes, or until the nuts begin to turn a richer color and smell aromatic. Remove and cool.

2. In a large skillet, heat the oil over medium heat. Add the garlic and cook 1 minute, stirring constantly. Add the chard in batches, stirring well, and cook 5 to 8 minutes, or until the chard is tender. Let cool.

3. Place the chard in a large strainer and place a smaller plate on top to press out all the excess liquid. Finely chop the drained chard. In a large bowl, whisk the egg. Add the drained chard, salt and pepper to taste, the cheese, and pine nuts. The stuffing can be made several hours ahead of time; cover and refrigerate until ready to stuff and roast the meat.

4. Place the butterflied meat on a clean work surface. Cover with a piece of waxed or parchment paper. Using a meat pounder or a heavy jar, gently pound the meat until it is flattened out evenly; you don't want the meat to be thin but pounded to an even thickness. Remove the paper.

5. Cut four or five 12-inch pieces of butcher's twine (or culinary string) and set aside.

6. Season the meat generously on both sides with salt and pepper. Spread the stuffing all over the inside surface of the meat (the side without the fat) except for 2 inches at the far end, pressing it down evenly. Roll up the meat into a fat long cigar shape, ending with the 2-inch section of meat that does not have the stuffing. Lift the meat (it's best if someone helps you with this) and tie it up widthwise with the twine.

The meat can be prepared an hour or two ahead of time up to this point; cover and refrigerate until ready to roast.

7. Place a rack in the middle of the oven and preheat to 400 degrees F. Place the stuffed lamb on a rack inside a medium, shallow roasting pan. Massage the oil onto the top of the meat and season again with salt and pepper. Roast for about 1 hour, or until a meat thermometer inserted in the meat (and not the stuffing) registers 140 degrees F for medium-rare. Let cool for about 5 minutes before slicing.

NOTE:
Ask your butcher to bone the lamb and give you the bone for a lamb stock or soup.

RACK OF LAMB WITH PISTACHIO-GARLIC-HERB CRUST AND ROASTED CHERRY TOMATOES

SERVES 2 TO 4

Rack of lamb is perfect holiday food—simple, elegant, and hard to mess up. We make a crust for the lamb using salty, crunchy pistachio nuts mixed with garlic, fresh rosemary, and thyme, and roast the meat surrounded by juicy cherry tomatoes (the only tomato worth eating in the winter). You can season the meat and pat the crust on top ahead of time and simply pop the meat in the oven about 45 minutes before you're ready to eat. Serve with roasted potatoes; Alabaster (page 86); Roasted Garlic, Herb, and Parmesan Custard (page 100); Roasted Acorn Squash and Beet Salad with Maple-Raisin Vinaigrette (page 19); or Winter Spinach Salad with Roasted Pears, Blue Cheese Toasts, and Dried Cranberry Vinaigrette (page 22), and crusty bread.

If you're serving a large crowd, you can buy two or three racks, but you'll need to increase the roasting time by 5 to 10 minutes.

INGREDIENTS

THE PISTACHIO-GARLIC-HERB CRUST

3 cloves garlic

⅓ cup (1 ounce) shelled pistachios

2 tablespoons chopped fresh rosemary

1 tablespoon fresh thyme

⅛ teaspoon salt

Generous grinding freshly ground black pepper

· · · · ·

1 rack of lamb (about 1½ pounds; 8 chops)

Salt

Freshly ground black pepper

2 cups cherry tomatoes

1 tablespoon olive oil

1 teaspoon finely chopped fresh rosemary

1 teaspoon finely chopped fresh thyme

1. Place a rack in the middle of the oven and preheat to 400 degrees F.

2. *Make the crust:* Put the garlic in the container of a food processor and pulse until finely chopped. Add the pistachios, rosemary, thyme, salt, and pepper and pulse until almost finely chopped. Set aside.

Continued...

...continued

3. Season the lamb with salt and pepper on both sides. Using your hands, press the crust onto the top of the lamb.

4. In a small bowl, toss together the tomatoes, oil, rosemary, thyme, and salt and pepper to taste until thoroughly combined.

5. Place the tomatoes in the bottom of a medium roasting pan, a large ovenproof skillet, or a large gratin dish. Gently place the lamb on top of the tomatoes, fat-side up. (The lamb can be prepared several hours ahead of time. Cover loosely, being careful of the crust, and refrigerate until ready to roast. Be sure to remove the meat 30 minutes before roasting to return it to room temperature.)

6. Roast the meat for 20 minutes. Raise the heat to 425 degrees F and roast another 10 to 18 minutes, or until the internal temperature of the lamb is 130 degrees for rare meat and 140 degrees for medium-rare.

7. Let the lamb sit for a few minutes before carving into separate chops. If the crust falls off during carving, simply spoon a portion back on top of each chop. Serve the tomatoes on the side along with the pan juices.

OSSO BUCO WITH ORANGE GREMOLATA

SERVES 4 TO 6

Rich and hearty, these braised veal shanks scream "winter comfort food."
We sauté leeks, celery, carrots, and garlic and then braise the veal shanks in red
wine and broth. The dish is finished off with an orange gremolata—a mixture
of grated orange and lemon zest, Italian parsley, and garlic. We love serving this
dish with the Orange-Scented Mashed Butternut Squash (page 89) or
the Mashed Parsnips and Pears (page 87).

This aromatic gremolata—an Italian classic—adds great flavor to soups
and stews, and can be sprinkled over salads, toast points, crostini, or
sautéed fish or meat dishes.

INGREDIENTS

1½ tablespoons olive oil

2 medium leeks, finely chopped

½ cup finely chopped celery
(about 1 large stalk)

½ cup finely chopped carrot
(about 1 large)

2 cloves garlic, minced

2 tablespoons minced
Italian parsley

2 thin strips lemon peel
(see Notes)

Salt

Freshly ground black pepper

1 cup all-purpose flour

5 pounds veal shanks
(about 4 large), cut into 2-inch
pieces (see Notes)

1½ tablespoons vegetable oil

1½ cups dry red wine

1½ cups beef broth

½ cup crushed Italian tomatoes

1 bay leaf

: : : : :

ORANGE GREMOLATA

¼ cup finely chopped fresh
Italian parsley

1 teaspoon minced garlic

2 teaspoons orange zest

½ teaspoon lemon zest

1. In a large pot, heat the olive oil over low heat. Add the leeks, celery, carrot, and half the garlic and cook, stirring occasionally, for 15 minutes. Add the remaining garlic, the parsley, lemon peel, and salt and pepper to taste, and cook another 5 minutes, until softened.

2. Place a rack in the middle of the oven and preheat to 325 degrees F.

3. Meanwhile, in a large bowl, mix the flour with some salt and pepper. Dredge the shanks in the seasoned flour, *Continued...*

…continued

coating well on all sides. In a large skillet, heat the vegetable oil over medium-high heat. Brown the shanks on all sides, 5 to 6 minutes. Drain on paper towels.

4. Raise the heat under the vegetable pot to high and let it heat up a minute. Add the wine and broth and bring to a boil. Reduce the heat to low and stir in the tomatoes and bay leaf. Place the shanks on top of the vegetables, gently pushing them down into the liquid.

5. Cover the pot and put it in the oven; bake about 1½ hours, basting once or twice. Check the stew and if the sauce seems very thin, open the lid slightly and cook another 15 to 20 minutes to reduce the juices. The veal should be very tender and just about falling off the bone. Taste for seasoning.

6. *Make the gremolata:* Mix together all the ingredients in a small bowl. The gremolata will keep, covered and refrigerated, for a day or two. Makes about ⅓ cup.

7. If you want a very sophisticated presentation, you can remove the shanks and place them in a deep bowl or serving platter. Strain the sauce on top of the veal to remove the vegetables. Sprinkle 2 tablespoons of the orange gremolata on top of the shanks, and serve the remaining gremolata on the side.

8. The osso buco can be made a day ahead of time up to this point. Cover and refrigerate until ready to serve. To reheat, place in a 325 degree F oven and heat for 15 to 20 minutes, until simmering hot.

NOTES:
Use a wide vegetable peeler to peel off the lemon zest from the whole lemon. Remove a shallow strip of just the yellow peel and not the bitter white pith.

Ask your butcher to cut the shanks into 2-inch pieces since they have large bones.

ROAST TURKEY WITH CRANBERRY-PECAN STUFFING

SERVES 10 TO 12, WITH LEFTOVERS

What do we love most about Thanksgiving? Well, you don't have to shop for presents. You don't have to decorate the house. And you don't have to go to the mall. But you do get to roast a turkey—one of the most delicious, overlooked birds that deserves to be cooked year-round rather than relegated to a single day.

We like to roast a big bird (about 18 to 20 pounds) because as far as we're concerned you can't have enough leftover turkey. (Think sandwiches, pot pies....) But you can easily halve the recipe for a smaller 8- to 10-pounder. Serve with the Holiday Orange-Cranberry Sauce (page 108), Apple Cider Jelly (page 110), Alabaster (page 86), Mashed Parsnips and Pears (page 87), and/or the Orange-Scented Mashed Butternut Squash (page 89), and give thanks.

INGREDIENTS

One 18- to 20-pound fresh turkey (preferably organic), at room temperature (see Notes)

1½ tablespoons vegetable oil

Salt

Freshly ground black pepper

2 batches Cranberry-Pecan Stuffing (page 103)

1 slice white or wheat bread

½ stick (¼ cup) unsalted butter

10 cloves garlic, peeled and left whole

2 tablespoons chopped fresh thyme

About 1 teaspoon sweet Hungarian paprika

::::::

THE GRAVY
1 turkey neck, giblets, and heart (reserved from the whole bird)

2 sweet yellow onions, quartered

2 ribs celery, chopped

2 carrots, chopped

½ cup coarsely chopped fresh Italian parsley

6 peppercorns

1 bay leaf

Salt

Freshly ground black pepper

2½ tablespoons all-purpose flour

Continued...

…continued

1. Preheat the oven to 450 degrees F. Arrange the oven rack so the bird will fit on the middle shelf without touching the top shelf.

2. Clean the bird and remove the neck, giblets, and heart, and set aside for the gravy. Pat the bird dry with paper towels. (The liver can be cooked separately; it is delicious lightly coated in flour and then sautéed in a hot skillet greased with 1 teaspoon of butter for about 5 to 6 minutes per side.)

3. Use the oil to lightly grease the bottom of a large roasting pan. Season the turkey with salt and pepper, inside the cavity and outside the skin. Loosely stuff both the body and neck cavities of the turkey with the stuffing, pressing down but being careful not to overstuff the bird. Use the whole slice of bread as a "door" to keep the stuffing inside the large body cavity; simply press the bread into the cavity as a way of keeping the stuffing inside so it won't fall out while roasting. Carefully place the bird into the roasting pan, breast-side up. If you want to use a roasting rack simply place the bird on the rack and set it inside the pan.

4. In a medium skillet, heat the butter over low heat. Add the garlic cloves and let cook 5 minutes, until the butter has completely melted and the garlic is just beginning to turn a light golden brown. Remove from the heat.

5. Using a spoon or a barbecue or pastry brush, brush the skin of the turkey with *some* of the garlic butter and scatter at least half the garlic cloves around and on top of the bird. *Keep the remaining garlic and butter for later basting.* Sprinkle the top of the bird with the thyme, paprika, and salt and pepper. Using a piece of kitchen string, tie the legs together to keep them from touching the sides of the roasting pan; tying the legs also makes for a "neater" looking roasted turkey. You can also tuck the wing tips behind the back of the bird, if you desire.

6. Place the roasting pan on the middle shelf and roast for 30 minutes. Reduce the heat to 350 degrees F and loosely cover the bird with foil. Roast the turkey another 3½ to 4½ hours, about 15 to 20 minutes per pound, depending on the freshness of the bird. (Fresh turkey tends to cook much faster than those that have been frozen.) Baste the bird every hour or so with the remaining garlic and butter and baste with the liquids that have accumulated on the bottom of the roasting pan. Remove the foil for the last hour of roasting time to give the bird a golden-brown glaze.

7. The bird should be a gorgeous golden brown; when

you wiggle a drumstick, it should feel slightly loose; and when you pierce the skin directly above the wing, the juice should run clear yellow, and not pink (see page 58 for more details on how to tell when the bird is properly cooked). The stuffing should be at least 160 degrees F in the center of the turkey. Gently remove the bird from the roasting pan and place on a serving platter; cover loosely with aluminum foil to keep warm.

8. *While the bird is roasting, begin the gravy:* Place the reserved neck, giblets, and heart in a medium saucepan (leave out the liver as it can make the stock cloudy). Add the onions, celery, carrots, parsley, peppercorns, bay leaf, and salt and pepper to taste to the pot and cover with about 6 cups cold water. Bring to a boil over high heat, reduce the heat, and let simmer on very low heat for about 1 to 2 hours. This will produce a light turkey stock that will be the basis of your gravy. Taste for seasoning and remove from the heat.

9. To finish the gravy, once you've removed the bird, place the roasting pan over two burners set on medium heat. (If there seems to be an excessive amount of turkey fat in the bottom of the pan, remove it by tilting the juices to the side and skim it off with a spoon or baster, being careful not to remove any of the natural juices.) Use a spatula to loosen any bits clinging to the bottom of the roasting pan. Sprinkle on the flour and, using a whisk, mix the flour with the juices in the bottom of the pan. Let cook 1 minute, stirring, until the paste has come together and is beginning to turn a pale golden color. Pour a little more than half (about 4 cups) of the turkey stock through a sieve into the pan and whisk to create a smooth gravy. Let simmer 5 to 10 minutes, until slightly thickened and flavorful. Thin the gravy by adding additional stock as needed. Season to taste with salt and pepper. Keep the gravy warm over low heat, stirring occasionally, until ready to serve.

10. Remove the stuffing from the bird and place it in a serving bowl; cover loosely to keep warm. Carve the bird and serve it with the stuffing and hot gravy on the side.

NOTES:
If the turkey is frozen be sure to defrost it in the refrigerator. Depending on the size, it can take up to 2 days to defrost thoroughly.

"Room temperature" simply means that the bird shouldn't come straight out of the refrigerator. You don't want to let the bird sit around for hours; remove it from the refrigerator about 1 hour before roasting while you make the stuffing.

SIMPLEST PORK ROAST

SERVES 6 TO 8

We love making pork roasts during the winter because they are so full of flavor and easy to prepare. Surround the roast with baby carrots and potatoes, if you like.

INGREDIENTS

One 8-rib bone-in Frenched pork rib roast (about 6 ½ to 8 pounds), tied

Salt

Freshly ground black pepper

1 cup panko or regular dried breadcrumbs

8 cloves garlic, peeled and minced

2 tablespoons chopped fresh rosemary

2 tablespoons chopped fresh thyme

2 tablespoons olive oil

1 tablespoon chopped fresh Italian parsley

1. Place a rack in the bottom third of the oven and preheat to 375 degrees F.

2. Place the pork on a roasting rack on a baking sheet with sides or a shallow roasting pan. Season liberally with the salt and pepper. Combine the remaining ingredients in a medium bowl, and stir to blend. Season the mixture with salt and pepper, and pack the breadcrumb mixture onto the fat side of the roast. (Remove any breadcrumbs that fall into the pan; they might burn.)

3. Roast the pork for 30 minutes, or until the breadcrumbs begin to brown. Cover the pork loosely with foil and roast another 1½ to 2 hours (about 2½ hours total), or until the pork reads 145 degrees F (for meat that is medium-rare) to 155 degrees F (for meat completely cooked through) in the center on an instant-read thermometer. Remove the foil and roast another 5 minutes, to brown the breadcrumbs.

4. Let the pork rest for 10 to 15 minutes at room temperature before carving. Serve with any breadcrumbs that fall off when slicing.

HOLIDAY HAM WITH MAPLE SYRUP–CLOVE-MARMALADE GLAZE

SERVES 8 TO 10, WITH LEFTOVERS

Glistening with marmalade and jeweled with fragrant cloves, this ham makes an impressive centerpiece. Figure about one pound of ham per person to make sure you have plenty of leftovers, because layered between two hearty slices of bread with a slab of Vermont Cheddar, the maple-sweetened slices make an excellent midnight sandwich.

INGREDIENTS

One 8- to 10-pound bone-in smoked ham (sliced or unsliced; see Note)

2 tablespoons whole cloves

2 large oranges

½ cup maple syrup

½ cup orange marmalade

1. Place a rack in the middle of the oven and preheat to 350 degrees F.

2. Trim the ham of any excess fat and place it flat-side down on a rack in a large roasting pan. Using a small, sharp knife, score the ham by making a grid pattern (¼ inch deep) across the ham at ¾-inch intervals. (If you're using a sliced ham, you'll only need to make 1 set of cuts, perpendicular to the slices that are already there.) Poke the pointy ends of the cloves into the ham where the lines intersect, scattering any remaining cloves on the bottom of the pan.

3. Zest the oranges, and set the zest aside in a small sauce-pan for the glaze. Juice the oranges directly over the ham, straining the seeds, then cover the ham with foil and bake for 2 hours, turning the pan and basting with the pan juices once or twice during cooking.

4. Meanwhile, add the syrup and marmalade to the pan with the zest, and bring to a simmer over low heat, stirring. When the marmalade has melted, remove from the heat and set aside.

5. After 2 hours, increase the oven temperature to 425 degrees F. Remove the foil, pour the glaze evenly over the ham, and bake another 30 minutes uncovered, or until nicely browned. Transfer the ham to a serving platter, and let it sit 15 minutes before slicing. Serve warm, drizzled with pan juices.

NOTE:
You can find smoked hams at specialty food shops and good butchers, or in most supermarkets. You can also use a honey-cured ham, sliced or unsliced.

VARIATIONS:
Substitute ½ cup cranberry or pomegranate juice for the orange juice.

Substitute a good-quality honey for the maple syrup.

ROAST SALMON AND SCALLOPS WITH ORANGE-CHAMPAGNE BEURRE BLANC

SERVES 6 TO 8

Sounds like a fancy title, we know. But don't be fooled into thinking this is a complicated recipe. Elegant and simple and ideal for any holiday dinner (we particularly like this for New Year's Eve), this salmon and scallop dish can be put together *almost* entirely ahead of time and roasted at the last minute. This is a perfect dish for non-beef eaters, or for a lighter change of pace at any holiday event.

The beurre blanc needs to be made while the fish is cooking; it doesn't hold up well if made ahead of time. Serve with Mashed Parsnips and Pears (page 87), Roasted Acorn Squash and Beet Salad with Maple-Raisin Vinaigrette (page 19), and Sharp Cheddar and Herb Popovers (page 107).

INGREDIENTS

2 ½ pounds salmon fillet

Salt

Freshly ground black pepper

2 teaspoons grated orange zest

1 cup all-purpose flour

1 ½ pounds sea scallops

1 ½ to 2 tablespoons olive oil

1 ½ cups Champagne or dry white wine

½ cup freshly squeezed orange juice

: : : : :

THE ORANGE-CHAMPAGNE BEURRE BLANC

⅓ cup Champagne or dry white wine

1 large shallot, minced (about 2 tablespoons)

2 teaspoons grated orange zest

¼ cup freshly squeezed orange juice (use the orange you zested)

2 sticks (1 cup) unsalted butter, cut into tablespoons

Salt

Freshly ground black pepper

1. Place the salmon in a large shallow roasting pan, baking dish, or ovenproof skillet (large enough to hold the salmon and the scallops). Season the salmon flesh with salt, pepper, and the orange zest.

2. Place the flour in a large bowl and season with salt and pepper. Dredge the scallops in the seasoned flour.

Continued...

. . . *continued*

3. Heat the oil in a large skillet over medium-high heat until hot. Sear the scallops for 1 to 1½ minutes on each side, or until golden. (The scallops should just be seared on the outside and not cooked through.) Remove to a plate. (If the skillet is dark or filled with little burnt pieces, remove from the heat and clean it out.)

4. Heat the skillet over high heat and add the 1½ cups Champagne; simmer for 5 minutes. Add the orange juice and cook another 2 minutes. Remove from the heat and add salt and pepper to taste. (The recipe can be made ahead of time up to this point; cover and refrigerate the salmon, seared scallops, and reduced Champagne/orange juice.)

5. Place a rack in the middle of the oven and preheat to 425 degrees F. Roast the salmon for 10 minutes.

6. If made ahead, reheat the Champagne–orange juice reduction over low heat until just simmering.

7. *Meanwhile, start the beurre blanc:* In a medium saucepan, mix together the ⅓ cup Champagne, shallot, zest, and orange juice. Bring to a boil over high heat. Reduce the heat to medium and simmer 8 to 10 minutes, or until reduced to about 2 tablespoons. Reduce the heat to low, add 4 tablespoons of the butter, and whisk until melted. Add the remaining butter, 1 tablespoon at a time, whisking continuously.

8. Remove from the heat and season with salt and pepper to taste. Pour the sauce through a fine-mesh sieve, pressing down on the shallots. Discard the shallots. The sauce should not be made ahead of time; keep it warm over very low heat.

9. Remove the salmon from the heat and arrange the seared scallops around the fish. Pour the hot reduced Champagne–orange juice sauce over the fish and roast for another 10 minutes, or until the salmon and scallops are opaque in the center. Serve the salmon and scallops drizzled with the pan juices. Serve the Orange-Champagne Beurre Blanc on the side.

BAKED PASTA WITH ROASTED WILD MUSHROOMS IN A CREAMY THYME SAUCE

SERVES 6

It's hard to explain how a dish this simple can be so elegant and delicious. Three types of wild mushrooms—portobello, shiitake, and cremini—are roasted at high heat, tossed with fresh thyme and cream, and then with a shaped pasta. We love serving this rich, comforting dish in large individual gratin dishes or ramekins (it's more special for a holiday meal). The pasta can be served as a first course, a main course (particularly good for vegetarians at large meat-laden holiday feasts), or as a comforting dinner anytime during the winter holidays. The pasta and sauce can be made several hours ahead of time, placed in individual ramekins, and baked just before serving.

INGREDIENTS

1 pound portobello mushrooms, stems trimmed, sliced or chopped into 1-inch pieces (see Note)

1 pound cremini mushrooms, stems trimmed, sliced or chopped into 1-inch pieces (see Note)

8 ounces shiitake mushrooms, stems trimmed, sliced or chopped into 1-inch pieces (see Note)

1 large sweet yellow onion, diced

¼ cup plus 2 tablespoons olive oil

2 tablespoons chopped fresh thyme or 2 teaspoons dried

4 cloves garlic, minced

Salt

Freshly ground black pepper

1 cup heavy cream

1 pound shaped pasta, like penne, farfalle (bows), rotelle (little corkscrew shapes), conchiglie (shells), fusilli (spirals), or ziti

1 cup grated Parmesan cheese

1. Place a rack in the middle of the oven and preheat to 425 degrees F.

2. In a rimmed baking sheet, tray, or large roasting pan, thoroughly combine the mushrooms, onion, ¼ cup of the olive oil, thyme, garlic, and a generous amount of salt and pepper. Roast for 10 minutes. Remove from the oven and gently stir. Roast another 5 minutes. Add the cream, stir well, and roast another 5 minutes, or until

Continued...

...continued
the cream begins to thicken and the mushrooms are tender. Remove from the oven and season with salt and pepper to taste.

3. Meanwhile, bring a large pot of lightly salted water to boil over high heat. Add the pasta and cook about 10 minutes, or until al dente or almost tender (the pasta will be baked as well so you don't want to overcook it). Drain. Place the pasta back in the pot and toss with the remaining 2 tablespoons oil, and salt and pepper to taste.

4. Pour the hot mushroom sauce on top of the pasta and gently mix. Add ¼ cup of the cheese and gently mix.

5. The pasta can be served in one large gratin dish or ovenproof baking dish, but it's much more elegant served in six individual (2-cup) gratin dishes or ramekins. Sprinkle the top of each ramekin or the large gratin dish with the remaining cheese. The dish(es) can be covered and refrigerated for several hours up to this point.

6. Bake the pasta in the 425 degree F oven for 5 to 10 minutes, depending on the size of the dish, or until it is hot and the cheese is bubbling.

NOTE: To clean the mushrooms, simply wipe the dirt off with a damp paper towel.

3

CHAPTER

SIDE
DISHES

ALABASTER: MASHED POTATOES AND TURNIPS

SERVES 6 TO 8

Turnips have a distinctive, earthy flavor that can be overwhelming when eaten on their own. They are the perfect balance to creamy potatoes, though, adding a touch of mystery to one of the most common holiday foods around. You can prepare the mashed turnips and potatoes hours ahead of time and reheat in a pot set over low heat, or in a gratin dish or ovenproof skillet at 350 degrees F for about 15 minutes, or until bubbling hot. You can make this dish using all low-fat milk or a combination of milk and cream, depending on how rich you want the dish to be.

INGREDIENTS

1 large turnip (about 2 pounds), peeled and chopped

2 ½ pounds Yukon Gold potatoes, peeled and chopped

2 to 3 tablespoons unsalted butter

About 1 ½ cups whole milk, low-fat milk, heavy cream, or a combination

¼ cup minced fresh chives or parsley (optional)

Salt

Freshly ground black pepper

1. Bring a large pot of lightly salted water to boil over high heat. Add the turnip and potatoes and cook for about 20 minutes, or until tender when tested with a small sharp knife. Drain well. Return the vegetables to the pot and let dry out for a minute or two over the warm burner.

2. Add the butter and about 1 cup of the milk and mash the vegetables using a hand-held masher or an immersion blender. It's fine for the mixture to be slightly chunky. Stir in the chives (if using) and season with salt and pepper to taste. Add the additional ½ cup milk or cream as needed for the desired consistency. Serve hot.

VARIATIONS:

Omit the turnip and add 2 pounds peeled, chopped parsnips.

Omit the turnip and add 1 leek, cut into 1-inch pieces, and 2 onions, peeled and chopped. Add the leek and onions after the potatoes have cooked for 10 minutes to avoid overcooking.

Omit the turnip and add a 2-pound winter squash, peeled and chopped.

Add 6 peeled whole garlic cloves to the pot with the potatoes and turnips for a garlic-flavored dish.

Place the mashed potatoes in a gratin dish and sprinkle with 1 cup grated hard cheese (Parmesan, Cheddar, Gruyère) or a soft goat cheese or blue cheese and bake for 30 minutes at 350 degrees F.

MASHED PARSNIPS AND PEARS

SERVES 8

Why is it we always serve plain old mashed potatoes or mashed sweet potatoes year after year? We decided to experiment with various vegetables and fruits that pair well and would make delicious accompaniments to any holiday roast. Sweet parsnips and pears turned out to be an excellent, unexpected combination.

INGREDIENTS

2 pounds small, thin parsnips, peeled and cut into ½-inch pieces

2 ripe pears, peeled, cored, and chopped into ½-inch pieces

⅔ cup heavy cream

3 tablespoons unsalted butter, cubed

Salt

Freshly ground black pepper

1. Bring a medium pot of water to a boil. Add the parsnips, cover, and cook for 10 to 12 minutes, or until tender when tested with a small, sharp knife. Drain thoroughly.

2. Place the cooked parsnips in the container of a food processor. Add the pears to the hot parsnips and whirl until chunky. Add the cream, butter, and salt and pepper to taste, and puree until almost smooth. The mixture can be slightly chunky, or you may prefer it smoother. Taste for seasoning.

3. Serve hot or make ahead of time and place in a small casserole or ovenproof skillet, cover, and refrigerate until ready to cook. To reheat, place in a 350 degree F oven for about 15 minutes, or until bubbling hot. Stir well before serving.

VARIATION:
Add 2 peeled, chopped apples to the puree instead of the pears.

ORANGE-SCENTED MASHED BUTTERNUT SQUASH

SERVES 4

This is a nice twist on mashed squash, where butternut squash is pureed with orange zest and juice for a deliciously sweet side dish.

INGREDIENTS

2 pounds peeled, seeded butternut squash, chopped into 1-inch pieces

¼ cup freshly squeezed orange juice

1 tablespoon unsalted butter, cubed

1 teaspoon honey

1 teaspoon orange zest

Salt

Freshly ground black pepper

1. Fill a large pot with 2 inches of lightly salted water and bring to a simmer over high heat. Add the squash, cover, reduce the heat to medium, and cook for 15 to 20 minutes, or until the squash is tender when pierced with a fork or small, sharp knife.

2. Drain the squash, and transfer it to the container of a food processor. Add the juice, butter, honey, zest, and salt and pepper to taste, and puree until smooth. Season again to taste.

3. The squash can be prepared ahead. Place finished squash in a casserole dish. Cover and refrigerate up to 2 days. To reheat, place in a 350 degree F oven, covered, for 30 minutes, or until warmed through.

VARIATIONS:
Try substituting acorn squash or your favorite winter squash for the butternut.

Add a large, peeled, chopped carrot to the pot with the squash.

Add a dash of ground nutmeg, allspice, or cinnamon to the puree.

FENNEL AND POTATO GRATIN

SERVES 8

The subtle anise flavor of fresh fennel gives this potato gratin a light, fresh taste.
Serve with any holiday roast.

INGREDIENTS

½ stick (¼ cup) unsalted butter, cubed, plus extra for greasing the pan

2 ½ pounds Yukon Gold potatoes, peeled and very thinly sliced

3 large bulbs fresh fennel, cored and thinly sliced

¼ cup all-purpose flour

2 tablespoons chopped fresh thyme or 1 ½ teaspoons dried

1 tablespoon chopped fresh rosemary or ½ teaspoon dried

Salt

Freshly ground black pepper

½ cup heavy cream

1 cup milk

½ cup grated Parmesan cheese

1. Lightly grease a large gratin dish (about 14 x 11 x 2 inches) with butter. Layer the bottom of the dish with half of the potatoes. Layer half of the fennel slices on top. Season with half of the flour, half of the thyme and rosemary, and salt and pepper to taste. Dot with half of the butter cubes. Repeat with the remaining potatoes, fennel, flour, thyme, rosemary, and butter, and season with salt and pepper to taste. (You can make the dish several hours ahead of time. Cover and refrigerate until ready to bake.)

2. Place a rack in the middle of the oven and preheat to 400 degrees F.

3. Pour the cream and milk on top of the gratin. Bake, covered, for 30 minutes. Tilt the dish and baste the milk and cream on top of the potatoes and fennel. Sprinkle the cheese on top of the gratin. Reduce the heat to 300 degrees F, leave uncovered, and bake for another 45 minutes to 1 hour, or until the potatoes and fennel are tender, the cheese melted, and almost all of the milk and cream have cooked into the vegetables. Let rest about 5 minutes before serving hot.

SWEET WINTER SQUASH GRATIN

SERVES 4 TO 6

Slices of bright orange winter squash are layered with sage and rosemary
and baked with maple syrup and a touch of heavy cream. Serve with any holiday
meat—turkey, chicken, pork, or beef—or on its own with a big winter salad
and crusty bread.

INGREDIENTS

1½ tablespoons butter, cubed

1½ pounds winter squash,
like butternut, peeled and cut
into ¼-inch slices

2 teaspoons chopped fresh
sage or ½ teaspoon dried

2 teaspoons chopped fresh
rosemary or ½ teaspoon dried

⅓ cup heavy cream

2 tablespoons maple syrup

Salt

Freshly ground black pepper

1. Place a rack in the middle of the oven and preheat to 400 degrees F.

2. Lightly grease the bottom of a medium gratin dish or ovenproof skillet with one of the small cubes of butter. Layer the squash slices on top, overlapping them slightly. Sprinkle the herbs evenly on the squash and pour the cream and syrup on top. Season liberally with salt and pepper.

3. Bake, basting the squash with the juices once or twice, for 45 to 50 minutes, or until the squash feels tender when tested with a small, sharp knife. Remove from the heat and let sit for a few minutes to let the juices settle before serving.

SAUTÉED BRUSSELS SPROUTS WITH NUTMEG-CARDAMOM CREAM AND PANCETTA BREADCRUMBS

SERVES 8

There are several elements we love in this dish. First the Brussels sprouts are thinly sliced and sautéed and then simmered with a boldly flavored nutmeg and cardamom cream. Diced pancetta—a cured, unsmoked Italian bacon—is tossed with crunchy panko breadcrumbs to create a fabulous topping. The whole dish can be prepared ahead of time and popped into the oven about 15 minutes before serving.

INGREDIENTS

3 tablespoons olive oil

2 shallots, finely chopped

1 clove garlic, minced

2 pounds Brussels sprouts, trimmed and cut into ¼-inch round slices

1 teaspoon ground nutmeg

½ teaspoon ground cardamom

Salt

Freshly ground black pepper

1½ cups heavy cream

THE PANCETTA-PANKO TOPPING

5 ounces pancetta or bacon

1 cup panko breadcrumbs

Pinch ground nutmeg

Pinch ground cardamom

Freshly ground black pepper

1. In a large skillet or 2 smaller skillets, heat the oil over low heat. Add the shallots and cook, stirring, for 4 minutes. Stir in the garlic and cook for 30 seconds. Add the Brussels sprouts and stir well. Add the nutmeg, cardamom, and salt and pepper to taste, and stir well. Cook for 4 minutes. Raise the heat to medium-low and add the cream. Let cook for 6 to 8 minutes, or until the cream simmers and begins

Continued...

. . . continued

to thicken slightly. Remove from the heat and taste for seasoning.

2. *Meanwhile, make the topping:* In another skillet, cook the pancetta over medium heat for 6 to 8 minutes, stirring frequently, until crisp on all sides. Remove from the heat and drain on paper towels. If using bacon, cook 4 to 8 minutes per side, depending on the thickness. Drain and cut into 1-inch pieces.

3. In a small bowl, mix together the cooked pancetta, panko, nutmeg, cardamom, and a generous grinding of pepper.

4. Pour the sprouts and cream into a large shallow gratin dish or casserole or an ovenproof skillet. Sprinkle the pancetta-panko mixture on top and press down lightly to create a crust. (The dish can be made several hours ahead of time up to this point. Cover and refrigerate until ready to serve.)

5. Place a rack in the middle of the oven and preheat to 350 degrees F. Bake the gratin for about 15 minutes, or until the cream is bubbling and the sprouts are hot.

VARIATIONS:
Omit the pancetta for a vegetarian version of the dish.

Add ½ cup crushed, chopped, or slivered almonds or your favorite nut to the topping.

THIN GREEN BEANS WITH BROWN BUTTER AND ROASTED CHESTNUTS

SERVES 8

Look for thin French-style green beans (called *haricots verts*) and vacuum-sealed bags of roasted chestnuts. The dish can be assembled and reheated just before serving.

INGREDIENTS

2 pounds thin green beans or haricots verts, ends trimmed

½ stick (¼ cup) unsalted butter

6 ounces peeled and roasted chestnuts, sliced

Salt

Freshly ground black pepper

1. Bring a large pot of water to a boil. Add the beans and simmer for 5 minutes, or until *almost* tender. Drain and place under cold running water to stop the cooking; drain again.

2. In a medium skillet, heat the butter over medium heat for about 4 minutes, until it sizzles and just begins to turn a rich brown. Remove from the heat and add the chestnut slices, and salt and pepper to taste, and cook over low heat for 2 minutes. Toss the brown butter and chestnuts with the green beans to thoroughly coat them all.

3. Serve immediately or place in a small casserole or shallow ovenproof dish, cover with foil, and refrigerate until ready to serve. Reheat the beans, covered, in a 350 degree F oven for about 15 minutes, or until hot.

VARIATIONS:

Substitute ¾ cup chopped or sliced nuts for the chestnuts.

Add ½ teaspoon grated lemon zest to the beans.

Add ⅓ cup cooked chopped bacon or pancetta to the beans.

Substitute 3 tablespoons of olive oil for the butter for a lighter version of the dish.

NOODLE KUGEL WITH RAISINS, APRICOTS, AND SLIVERED ALMONDS

SERVES 10

Like a savory/sweet quiche, this rich, hearty dish is traditionally served at Chanukah and other Jewish holidays. Egg noodles are mixed with a combination of eggs, sour cream, cottage cheese, cinnamon, and dried fruit, and then baked. Serve with Brisket with Winter Vegetables (page 59), Beef Tenderloin with Horseradish Crust, Roasted Potatoes, and Garlic (page 53), and other holiday meals. Kugel is delicious served reheated the next day or at room temperature with a good winter salad like Winter Radicchio Slaw (page 14) or Winter Spinach Salad with Roasted Pears, Blue Cheese Toasts, and Dried Cranberry Vinaigrette (page 22).

INGREDIENTS

1 stick (½ cup) unsalted butter, melted, plus extra for greasing the pan

Salt

1 pound wide egg noodles

4 large eggs

3 cups sour cream

2 cups large-curd cottage cheese

2 cups milk

¼ cup sugar

1 teaspoon ground cinnamon

¾ cup raisins

½ cup dried apricots, thinly sliced (optional)

⅔ cup (2 ounces) slivered almonds

1. Place a rack in the middle of the oven and preheat to 350 degrees F. Butter a large glass or ceramic ovenproof dish (about 13½ x 9½ inches wide).

2. Bring a large pot of salted water to a boil. Cook the noodles for about 12 minutes, until just tender. Drain.

3. Meanwhile, in a large bowl, whisk together the eggs. Whisk in the sour cream, cottage cheese, milk, melted butter, sugar, and half of the cinnamon until well mixed.

Add the raisins, apricots (if using), and half of the almonds and mix well.

4. Place the noodles in the baking dish and pour the egg mixture on top. Gently stir to make sure all the noodles are well coated. Sprinkle the top with the remaining almonds and cinnamon.

5. Bake the kugel for 1 hour, until it is a pale golden brown and the liquid has been cooked and absorbed. Let cool 5 minutes before cutting into small squares and serving.

ROASTED GARLIC, HERB, AND PARMESAN CUSTARD

SERVES 6

This is just the sort of side dish or first course you crave during the holidays—something with a large "Wow" factor that requires very little time or effort. These savory custards have a silky, creamy texture with the rich taste of roasted garlic, herbs, and cheese. They are a perfect accompaniment to roast beef, lamb, or poultry, or can be served as a first course or on top of an assortment of mixed greens.

The custards can be baked ahead of time and kept, covered, in the refrigerator for several hours. To reheat, carefully wrap the custards in foil and heat in a 350 degree F oven for 5 to 8 minutes, or until warm.

INGREDIENTS

Vegetable spray for the muffin pan

1 head garlic, ¼ inch cut off the top to just expose the cloves

1 tablespoon olive oil

2 large eggs

1 large egg yolk

1 teaspoon chopped fresh thyme or ½ teaspoon dried

1 teaspoon chopped fresh rosemary or ½ teaspoon dried

Salt

Freshly ground black pepper

½ cup heavy cream

¼ cup low-fat milk

⅓ cup grated Parmesan cheese

1. Place a rack in the middle of the oven and preheat to 350 degrees F. Spray 6 muffin cups or ramekins with the vegetable spray, making sure to grease the bottom and sides of the cups.

2. Place the garlic in a small ovenproof skillet and pour the oil on top. Roast for 20 to 25 minutes, depending on the size of the garlic, or until the cloves feel soft when you gently press them. Remove from the oven and let cool for 5 minutes. Squeeze the cloves out of the skins.

3. In the container of a food processor, pulse the roasted garlic until almost smooth. Add the eggs, egg yolk, herbs, and salt and pepper to taste, and process until well blended. With the motor still running, add the cream and milk and blend until smooth. Add the cheese and blend another 30 seconds.

4. Bring a medium pot of water to a boil.

Continued...

. . . continued

5. Place the prepared muffin pan in a large shallow roasting pan. Divide the custard mixture between the prepared cups. Pour enough boiling water into the roasting pan to come almost halfway up the sides of the muffin pan. Loosely cover the top of the pan with foil.

6. Bake the custards for about 25 minutes, or until the centers feel just firm to the touch. Remove the muffin pan from the roasting pan and let the custards cool down for a minute or two.

7. Serve the custard in the ramekin or use a flat kitchen knife to loosen the custards from the sides and bottoms of the pan. Place a large plate over the pan and carefully invert to release the custards. Serve warm or at room temperature.

CRANBERRY-PECAN STUFFING

SERVES 8 TO 10

We love all kinds of stuffing, but this one bursts with the fresh flavors of the season. Start collecting bread several days before you want to make the stuffing. Two-day-old bread is perfect (a bit crusty, but not too old) and remember that the more varieties of bread you use—white, whole-wheat, rye, marble, French, Italian, cornbread, ciabatta—the better.

There's enough stuffing here for a 10- to 12-pound turkey; if you want to use this stuffing for the Roast Turkey (page 71), you'll need to double it. Place any leftover stuffing in a well-greased casserole. It's also a delicious stuffing for chicken, duck, or Cornish hens, or served as a side dish to any holiday or simple family meal.

INGREDIENTS

2 tablespoons unsalted butter

1 tablespoon olive oil

3 medium Vidalia or sweet yellow onions, chopped

6 cloves garlic, thinly sliced

2 tablespoons chopped fresh thyme or 2 teaspoons dried

Salt

Freshly ground black pepper

5 stalks celery, chopped

½ cup very thinly sliced fresh basil leaves

1½ cups chopped fresh parsley

10 cups cubed bread (see headnote)

1 cup dried cranberries, cherries, or tomatoes

1 cup (3½ ounces) pecan halves or other nuts, coarsely chopped

1 to 1½ cups milk

1. In a large skillet, heat 1 tablespoon of the butter and the oil over medium-low heat. When the butter has melted and begins to sizzle, add the onions and garlic and cook, stirring, for about 8 minutes, or until the onions are soft. Season with half of the thyme and some salt and pepper. Add the celery, half of the basil, and half of the

Continued...

...continued

parsley, and cook for 5 minutes, stirring frequently, or until the celery is just beginning to soften. The celery should still have somewhat of a crunch.

2. Meanwhile, place the bread in a large bowl, and mix in the remaining thyme, basil, parsley, the dried cranberries, and pecans. Pour the celery mixture from the skillet on top of the bread and gently toss to mix all of the ingredients.

3. Place the skillet back over low heat and add the milk and the remaining 1 tablespoon butter and simmer for 2 to 4 minutes, using a spatula to scrape up any bits and pieces clinging to the bottom of the skillet. Pour 1 cup of the hot milk mixture over the bread and toss; the stuffing should be somewhat moist. If the stuffing seems dry, add the remaining ½ cup milk. Season to taste.

4. If making the stuffing more than an hour ahead of time, cover and refrigerate until you are ready to stuff the bird. The stuffing can also be placed in a lightly greased baking dish or casserole and baked at 350 degrees F for about 20 minutes, or until hot throughout. If possible, baste with some of the turkey juices from the bottom of the turkey pan to keep the stuffing moist.

VARIATIONS:

Add 1 dozen freshly shucked oysters (and their juices) to the skillet when the celery is cooking and cook for about 1 minute. They add a rich, briny flavor.

Add 1 pound sweet sausage (taken out of the casing) to the skillet along with the onions and cook for about 8 minutes, stirring well to break up the sausage into small pieces, until golden brown.

Add 1 cup roasted, coarsely chopped chestnuts instead of, or in addition to, the pecans.

SHARP CHEDDAR AND HERB POPOVERS

MAKES 9 TO 12 POPOVERS

Jonathan found the recipe for these gorgeously puffed, golden brown popovers laced with sharp Cheddar cheese and herbs. We would tell you they're addictive but that's a cliché. You've been warned.

The only trick here is that the popovers must be served as soon as they come out of the oven. Make a double batch and plan on having the first batch come out as you sit down to eat. Put the second batch in immediately and you'll have hot seconds to offer 40 minutes later. If you don't have a heavy, deep popover pan you can use a muffin pan, but you won't get the full rise and dramatic results. Serve with Standing Rib Roast Studded with Garlic (page 55) or Roast Turkey with Cranberry-Pecan Stuffing (page 71). They also make an excellent accompaniment to a winter salad and a cup of soup for a warming winter meal.

INGREDIENTS

2 cups whole or 2% milk

4 large eggs

¼ chopped mixed fresh herbs (we use rosemary, thyme, sage, and chives, but any combination will work)

⅛ teaspoon salt

Freshly ground black pepper

2 cups all-purpose flour

Vegetable spray for the pans

About 1½ cups grated sharp Cheddar, Gruyère, Parmesan, or your favorite hard grating cheese

1. Place a rack in the middle of the oven and preheat to 350 degrees F.

2. Place 1 large or 2 small popover pans in the preheated oven (you'll need 12 cups total).

3. Meanwhile, heat the milk in a small saucepan over low heat for 3 to 4 minutes, or until warm to the touch. Whisk the eggs, herbs, salt, and a generous grinding of pepper together in a large bowl. Add the warm milk while whisking to keep the milk from cooking the eggs. Sift the flour into the milk mixture and whisk well.

4. Remove the pan(s) from the oven and spray with vegetable spray, making sure the entire cups are well coated (popovers love to stick if you're not fastidious). Fill each of the cups three-fourths full and sprinkle about 1 heaping tablespoon of cheese on top of each.

5. Bake for 15 minutes. Carefully turn the pans from front to back and continue baking for another 25 minutes, or until the popovers have risen and are golden brown. Serve immediately.

HOLIDAY ORANGE-CRANBERRY SAUCE

MAKES ABOUT 6 CUPS

This is the classic sauce for accompanying a holiday turkey. Our version is loaded with oranges—fresh orange juice, orange zest, and thin strips of orange rind—candied ginger strips, and crunchy nuts. We also love to serve this sauce over pound cakes and butter cakes, as a dip for butter cookies, spread on morning toast and muffins and pancakes, or in a cranberry-Cheddar sandwich. Of course the ultimate use is on a leftover turkey sandwich with stuffing and crunchy lettuce on toasted white or whole-wheat bread.

INGREDIENTS

1¼ cups sugar

⅓ cup maple syrup

1 pound fresh cranberries

¼ cup freshly squeezed orange juice (see Notes)

¼ cup julienned orange rind (see Notes)

1 tablespoon grated orange zest (see Notes)

1 cup (3½ ounces) walnuts, pecans, or your favorite nut, coarsely chopped

2 tablespoons coarsely chopped candied (or crystallized) ginger (see Notes)

1. Combine the sugar and 2 cups of water in a large saucepan and bring to a boil over high heat. Reduce the heat to low and cook for 10 to 15 minutes, or until the sugar syrup begins to thicken slightly and turns a pale amber color.

2. Add the maple syrup and cranberries and cook, stirring occasionally, until the cranberries begin to pop.

3. Add the orange juice, rind, and zest and cook for another 5 to 10 minutes, or until the sauce begins to thicken *slightly*.

4. Remove the sauce from the heat and add the nuts and ginger, stirring well. Let cool completely.

5. Pour into a clean glass jar and cover; refrigerate for up to 1 week, or freeze for 6 months.

NOTES:
You'll need 2 or 3 large oranges. First, use 1 orange to remove the rind (the outer peel without the bitter white pith) by slicing it off with a small, sharp knife or a wide vegetable peeler. Use another orange to grate the rind for zest and then squeeze both oranges for their juice.

Candied or crystallized ginger is available in the specialty food section of most supermarkets or at chocolate or candy shops.

APPLE CIDER JELLY

MAKES ABOUT 1 CUP

There are some recipes that seem to have more in common with magic than plain old, everyday cooking. Apples have lots of natural pectin, so we wondered what would happen if you simmered down an entire gallon of good apple cider? The answer is you are left with a gorgeous amber-colored natural apple cider jelly. The only catch—this is true *slow cooking*—is that it can take up to three hours to transform one gallon of cider into about a cup of jelly, but trust us when we say it's well worth the time. Making the jelly is a great project when you're already in the kitchen baking cookies or other holiday foods.

Serve the jelly as a condiment with holiday roasts—we particularly like it with roast pork, lamb, and beef—or on your morning muffins and toast, with squash dishes, and even on top of butter cookies. Make a few batches and give the cider jelly as a gift (see page 117).

INGREDIENTS

1 gallon unpasteurized apple cider, with no additives

Place the cider in a large, heavy pot and bring to a gentle boil over high heat. Reduce the heat to low and let simmer for about 2 hours. After about 2 hours, the cider will begin to thicken and coat the back of a spoon. *This is the time to pay attention.* Keep cooking over a gentle simmer, on *very* low heat, for another 45 minutes or until the jam begins to thicken and the syrupy mixture comes to about 190 degrees F on a candy thermometer. Our jelly usually takes almost 3 hours to thicken. Let cool and place in a glass jelly jar. Refrigerate. The jelly will keep for several weeks.

VARIATIONS:

Make a chile-spiced apple cider jelly: Wrap a chile pepper (that is cut in half, lengthwise) in a piece of cheesecloth and tie it up. Place the chile in the cider for the first hour of cooking and then remove.

Make a mulled apple cider jelly: Wrap 1 cinnamon stick, 1 allspice berry, and 3 cloves in a piece of cheesecloth and tie it up tightly. Place in the cider during the first hour of cooking, then remove.

Make an herbal apple cider jelly: Add several fresh sage leaves or any fresh herb leaves during the first hour of cooking, then remove.

DESSERTS

ANDREA'S CHOCOLATE-DIPPED BUTTERCRUNCH

SERVES 6 TO 8

Kathy's sister-in-law, Andrea Gunst, shared this buttercrunch recipe with her several years ago and it has changed Kathy's holiday traditions forever. This is the stuff everyone begs for year after year, so be sure to make multiple batches. Buttercrunch, a caramel coated in chocolate and ground nuts, keeps for over a week and makes a great gift (see page 117).

You can double the recipe if you like, but if you want to make more you shouldn't try to multiply the recipe by three or four—simply keep making double batches.

INGREDIENTS

2 sticks (1 cup) unsalted butter

1 cup sugar

1 tablespoon light corn syrup

2 large (7- or 8-ounce) chocolate bars (see Notes)

About 1 cup (3 ½ ounces) very finely chopped walnuts (see Notes)

1. Line a cookie sheet with sides with a piece of well-greased aluminum foil.

2. In a medium saucepan, heat the butter, sugar, corn syrup, and 2 tablespoons of water over low heat, stirring frequently. The mixture will caramelize and is ready when it hits 290 degrees F on a candy thermometer. Watch it carefully, particularly toward the end of the cooking process. It will take at least 15 to 20 minutes to reach 290 degrees on low heat. The mixture can burn easily; reduce the heat to very low and stir constantly if it seems to be cooking too quickly or turning darker than pale golden brown.

3. When the candy hits 290 degrees F, remove from the heat and carefully spread it out in an even layer on the sheet of greased foil. Spread quickly with a spatula to make a fairly thin layer.

Continued...

...continued

Let cool and harden. (If you are really impatient you can place the cookie sheet outside in the cold in a protected place so it will harden more quickly.)

4. While the buttercrunch is hardening, melt the chocolate in a double boiler (or in a metal bowl set over a pan of barely simmering water), stirring constantly until smooth. If you choose to let the buttercrunch harden outside or in a very cold spot, you must bring it back to room temperature before spreading with the chocolate. If the buttercrunch is too cold or hot, the chocolate won't adhere properly.

5. When the buttercrunch is hard to the touch (you shouldn't feel any soft spots), use a soft spatula and spread a thin layer of chocolate over the entire thing. Sprinkle with half the nuts, pressing down lightly so they adhere. Again, if you are the impatient type, you can let the chocolate harden in a cold spot. The chocolate should be fully dry—no wet spots to the touch.

6. Use a second cookie sheet, and place it on top of the chocolate. Gently flip the buttercrunch over and carefully peel away the foil from the candy. Spread the remaining chocolate on top of the other side of the buttercrunch. Sprinkle with the remaining nuts, pressing down lightly. Let the chocolate harden and set in a cool spot.

7. When the buttercrunch is dry and hard, break it into small pieces. You can keep it in a cool, dry tin or tightly sealed plastic bag for about 2 weeks.

NOTES:

Buttercrunch can be made successfully with regular grocery-store milk chocolate or chocolate chips, but you can also splurge and use fabulous bittersweet or semisweet 60% cacao chocolate. The choice is yours.

You can use walnuts, almonds, pecans, pistachios, or any type of nut, but they must be finely chopped to adhere properly to the chocolate.

For friends and family who love to cook (or simply love to eat), there is no finer gift than something from the kitchen. It can be as simple as a batch of cookies or homemade buttercrunch, or you could make up a double batch of soup for a friend (one to eat right away and one to freeze). Wrap the gift with a new piece of kitchen equipment (see ideas below) or add the recipe. There is so much more meaning in a gift that was made with your hands and heart than one from a mall.

* Pour **Butternut Squash Soup** (page 28) into a clean glass jar, add a note about refrigerating or freezing the soup, and include a batch of **Curried Maple Pecans** (page 49). Add a brand new immersion blender.

* **Curried Maple Pecans** (page 49) can be wrapped tightly in a plastic bag and then wrapped in tissue paper. Add a note about the various uses: sprinkled on salads, soups, stews, served with cocktails, etc. Wrap the nuts in a new serving bowl or basket.

* Buy a friend a new popover pan and share the recipe for **Sharp Cheddar and Herb Popovers** (page 107).

* **Gremolata** (page 67) can be made up and placed in small glass bowls that can be used for serving it and other spice mixtures.

Cover and wrap up, adding a note explaining all the uses: sprinkled on soups and stews, sautéed fish and meat, etc.

* Put the **Apple Cider Jelly** (page 110) in a clear glass jar, covered in raffia ribbons. Add a note about how to use it and store it.

* The **Vanilla Bean Caramel Sauce** (page 130) makes a great gift. Wrap it up in a clear squeeze bottle (which you can find at any kitchen supply shop or in the grocery store; they are generally used for mustard and ketchup) and be sure to include a note with the recipe.

* **Holiday Orange-Cranberry Sauce** (page 108) will keep a week in a glass jar or frozen for 3 months. Add a jar of crystallized ginger as an extra treat.

* **Buttercrunch** (page 114) will keep for about 2 weeks if kept in a cool spot. Wrap in a tightly sealed bag and place in a new ramekin or glass or ceramic bowl and cover with tissue paper.

* **Orange-Ginger Shortbread** (page 122) can be wrapped in a new bowl, an olive boat (one of those long, cylinder-shaped plates that olives are traditionally served in), or wrapped up in tissue paper. It will keep about 1 week.

POACHED PEARS WITH CHAMPAGNE-GINGER-CINNAMON SYRUP

SERVES 4

Pears are sexy and voluptuous—the sophisticated fall cousins to the apple. Here we poach the pears in a mixture of Champagne, fresh ginger, and cinnamon and then simmer the mixture down to create an aromatic syrup. The pears can be made a day ahead of time and chilled overnight.

INGREDIENTS

4 barely ripe Bosc pears

3 cups Champagne or sparkling wine

1 cup sugar

¼ cup roughly chopped, peeled fresh ginger

2 cinnamon sticks

1. Peel the pears, leaving the stems attached. Working from the bottom of the pears, use a small melon baller (or small, sharp knife) to scoop out the cores. Cut a very thin slice off the bottom of the pears so they sit flat on a surface.

2. Combine the Champagne, 1 cup water, the sugar, ginger, and cinnamon in a saucepan large enough to hold the pears snugly lying down. Bring to a simmer over medium heat, stirring occasionally. When all the sugar has dissolved, add the pears.

3. Lower the heat, cover the pears with a round of parchment paper cut to fit the pan, then with a small plate. (This prevents the pears from bobbing up and out of the liquid.) Simmer for 30 to 45 minutes, or until the pears are soft when gently poked with a small knife or wooden skewer.

4. Transfer the pears to a platter and tent with foil to keep them moist and warm. Bring the poaching liquid to a boil, and cook for about 20 minutes, or until the liquid reduces to about 2 cups and becomes thicker and almost syrupy. Let cool slightly, then strain. Serve the pears warm, chilled, or at room temperature, drizzled with the syrup.

VARIATIONS:
Add ¼ teaspoon crushed saffron threads to the Champagne mixture. It will add a gorgeous saffron-orange color and a pleasing, exotic flavor.

Add a vanilla bean to the Champagne mixture, cut in half lengthwise.

FOUR-BERRY CRISP

SERVES 6 TO 8

We are all about cooking food that is fresh, local, and seasonal. But sometimes frozen fruit works just as well, particularly in the winter when bright colors and fresh fruit are a rarity. In this crisp, we combine frozen cranberries, blueberries, strawberries, and raspberries, and top them off with a hazelnut, cinnamon, and ginger crust. The crisp is best served warm straight from the oven, topped with ice cream (try ginger ice cream), yogurt, whipped cream, or crème fraîche, but it can also be made ahead of time and reheated at 250 degrees F for about 20 minutes, or until warm and bubbling.

INGREDIENTS

1 pound frozen blueberries

1 pound frozen strawberries

1 pound frozen raspberries

¾ cup frozen or fresh cranberries

⅔ cup granulated sugar

1¼ cups all-purpose flour

2½ teaspoons ground ginger

1 cup (3½ ounces) chopped hazelnuts

¾ cup old-fashioned rolled oats

¾ cup packed dark brown sugar

¾ teaspoon ground cinnamon

Pinch salt

7 tablespoons unsalted butter, melted

1. Place a rack in the middle of the oven and preheat to 375 degrees F.

2. In a large bowl, gently combine all the fruit with the granulated sugar, ½ cup of the flour, and 1 teaspoon of the ginger until the flour coats all the pieces. Transfer to a large 9-x-13-inch baking or gratin dish, and bake for 20 minutes.

3. Meanwhile, in the same bowl, stir together the hazelnuts, oats, brown sugar, cinnamon, salt, and remaining ¾ cup flour and 1½ teaspoons ginger to blend. Drizzle the melted butter over the top, and stir until all the ingredients are moistened.

4. After 20 minutes, gently stir to combine the berries and sprinkle on the topping in an even layer, gently pushing it all the way to the edges of the pan. Bake another 30 to 40 minutes, or until the topping is browned and the filling is bubbling.

VARIATIONS:

Use fresh berries and reduce the baking time by 5 to 10 minutes.

Substitute pistachios, walnuts, or almonds for the hazelnuts.

Add a pinch of allspice or cardamom to the topping.

ORANGE-GINGER SHORTBREAD

MAKES ABOUT 6 DOZEN COOKIES

Around the holidays, cookies are everywhere. What we like about these shortbreads is that they have a light, fresh taste, and are a refreshing change from the same ol' butter cookies that everyone seems to make this time of year. Serve the shortbread with coffee or hot cocoa, or as part of a holiday dessert buffet. The shortbreads hold up well for almost a week and make a great gift (see page 117). The dough can also be tightly wrapped in foil and frozen for several months.

INGREDIENTS

4 sticks (2 cups) unsalted butter, at room temperature

½ cup confectioners' sugar

⅓ cup granulated sugar

4 cups all-purpose flour, plus a bit more for pulling dough together

3 navel oranges, zested

2 teaspoons grated (or very finely chopped) fresh ginger

1 teaspoon ground ginger

½ teaspoon salt

1. In a standing mixer fitted with the paddle attachment (or using a hand-held electric mixer), beat the butter with both sugars on medium speed for 3 to 4 minutes, scraping down the sides of the bowl and the paddle when necessary, until light and fluffy.

2. Meanwhile, whisk the 4 cups of flour, the orange zest, fresh ginger, ground ginger, and salt together in a bowl. With the machine on low speed, add the flour mixture about 1 cup at a time, mixing between each addition until just combined, and scraping the sides of the mixing bowl when necessary.

3. Place the dough on a clean surface lightly dusted with flour. Gently knead the dough until it comes together (it should feel sticky). Divide the dough in half.

4. Working with one section at a time, shape the dough into a log about 1½ inches in diameter. Wrap the dough in plastic or parchment paper, and refrigerate until very firm, at least 2 hours or overnight.

(The dough can also be well wrapped and frozen up to 1 month. To bake, thaw at room temperature until warm enough to cut, and then bake as directed.)

5. Place a rack in the middle of the oven and preheat to 300 degrees F. Line 2 large baking sheets with parchment paper. Slice 1 dough log into ¼-inch-thick pieces, and place the cookies about ¾ inch apart on the baking sheets (one log should fill both baking sheets). Bake for 20 to 25 minutes, rotating the sheets from top to bottom and end to end halfway through baking, until the cookies are firm and just barely beginning to brown at the edges.

6. Let the cookies cool 5 minutes on the baking sheets, then transfer them carefully to cooling racks to cool completely. Store in airtight containers up to 1 week.

VARIATIONS:
Substitute lemon or Meyer lemon for the orange.

Add 1 tablespoon chopped crystallized ginger to the dough for a super-ginger flavor.

VANILLA BEAN CHEESECAKE WITH CHOCOLATE CRUST

SERVES 12

Rich, creamy cheesecake is the perfect dessert for any holiday meal.
This one is perfumed with fresh vanilla beans and made with a simple chocolate
cookie crust—a study in black and white. We like to serve it with Vanilla Bean
Caramel Sauce (page 130). The cake can be made, covered and refrigerated,
a day before serving.

INGREDIENTS

1 stick (½ cup) unsalted butter, plus more for greasing the pan

One 9-ounce package chocolate wafer cookies

1¼ cups plus 2 tablespoons sugar

2 pounds cream cheese, at room temperature

One 3-inch vanilla bean

4 large eggs, at room temperature

Vanilla Bean Caramel Sauce (optional)

1. Grease a 10-inch spring-form pan with butter.

2. Place the cookies in a food processor and process until very finely chopped, like breadcrumbs. Measure out 2¼ cups and reserve any left-over for another use.

3. Melt the 1 stick of butter in a small saucepan over low heat. Remove it from the heat and add the cookie crumbs and 2 tablespoons of the sugar, and stir until well blended. Pour the cookie mixture into the springform pan and use your hands to pat it firmly into an even layer on the bottom of the pan. Refrigerate the crust at least 15 minutes, and up to 24 hours.

4. Place a rack in the middle of the oven and preheat to 350 degrees F. Wrap the bottom of the cake pan in aluminum foil, and place it on a baking sheet. (This prevents a mess, in case your pan—like many springform pans—is leaky.) Set aside.

5. In the work bowl of a standing mixer fitted with

the paddle attachment, combine the cream cheese and the remaining 1¼ cups sugar, and scrape the seeds from the vanilla bean on top. Whip on medium speed for about 4 minutes, until light and fluffy, scraping down the bowl and paddle when necessary. Add the eggs one at a time, scraping the sides down between each addition.

6. Pour the batter into the pan, and bake for 60 to 70 minutes, or until the cake wiggles as one piece when you shake it gently. (It may still look a little soft in the center.) If the cake starts to brown, place a cookie sheet on the shelf above it to prevent it from coloring. Let cool for 30 minutes before removing the cake from the pan.

7. Serve immediately, or chill overnight. Serve with the Vanilla Bean Caramel Sauce, if desired.

VARIATIONS:
Use amaretti (almond) cookies for the crust instead of chocolate cookies.

Serve with lemon curd.

Serve with Holiday Orange-Cranberry Sauce (page 108).

CARAMEL-COVERED APPLE GALETTE

SERVES 4 TO 6

This galette looks like a rustic French tart, with the sweet, tart flavor of apples and a simple caramel sauce on top. The galette can be served immediately from the oven or made ahead of time. Reheat for 10 minutes in a 325 degree F oven and then top with the caramel just before serving.

INGREDIENTS

3 crisp-tart apples, peeled, cored, and cut into thin slices (¼ inch at thickest side)

½ lemon, juiced

2 tablespoons all-purpose flour

2 tablespoons sugar, plus more for dusting crust

1 teaspoon ground cinnamon

½ recipe Sweet Pie Pastry (page 131), chilled

¼ cup Vanilla Bean Caramel Sauce (page 130)

1. Place a rack in the middle of the oven and preheat to 400 degrees F. Line a baking sheet with parchment paper or a silicone baking mat and set aside.

2. In a large bowl, mix the apples with the lemon juice and set aside. In a small bowl, blend the flour, 2 tablespoons sugar, and cinnamon together.

3. Roll the pastry dough out into a circle about ¼ inch thick and 10 inches in diameter. Transfer the crust to the baking sheet. Sprinkle about half of the flour/sugar mixture onto the center of the crust, leaving the outer 2 inches empty. Mix the rest of the flour/sugar mixture into the apples, and stir to blend. Pile the apples into the center of the crust, over the flour/sugar (or arrange in concentric circles, if you have the patience). Fold the empty edges of the crust up and over the apples in roughly 4-inch sections, using your hands to press each section onto the preceding layer of dough. (You can also use a little water to help the dough stick together.) If the dough is soft, refrigerate for 30 minutes, until firm.

4. Sprinkle the dough with additional sugar, and bake for 50 to 60 minutes, or until the crust is golden brown and the apples are soft and browned on top. Let cool 10 minutes on the baking sheet, then transfer to a serving platter and drizzle the entire apple section and some crust with the caramel sauce.

VARIATION:
Toss ⅛ cup chopped crystallized ginger with the apples.

PECAN PIE WITH CARAMEL SAUCE

SERVES 6

What are the holidays without pecan pie? We wanted to give this classic a slightly new spin without making it too sweet. We drizzle on a simple caramel sauce, which can be made days ahead of time and goes well with virtually everything (cakes, pies, cookies, ice cream…). If you can find a squeeze bottle (the kind they use to serve ketchup and mustard at diners) you can squeeze the caramel onto the pie in a nice pattern.

INGREDIENTS

½ recipe Sweet Pie Pastry (page 131), chilled

2 large eggs

½ cup light corn syrup

⅓ cup packed light brown sugar

½ teaspoon vanilla extract

1 ¾ cups (5 ½ ounces) pecan halves

1 recipe Vanilla Bean Caramel Sauce (page 130)

1. Place a rack in the middle of the oven and preheat to 375 degrees F.

2. Roll out the pastry on a lightly floured surface and line a round 9-inch tart pan. Place it on a cookie sheet.

3. In a large bowl, whisk together the eggs. Add the corn syrup, sugar, and vanilla and beat well. Add the pecans and pour the mixture into the pie shell. Bake for about 45 minutes, or until a toothpick inserted in the center comes out clean. Let cool completely.

4. Drizzle the pie with the caramel sauce in a crisscross pattern. Serve any remaining caramel sauce on the side. *Continued…*

...*continued*

VANILLA BEAN CARAMEL SAUCE

MAKES ABOUT 1 CUP

Making caramel—the act of melting sugar over high heat and then mixing it with other ingredients— used to scare us so much that we avoided it altogether. But after many experiments we came up with this simple, no-fail recipe. Remember: There is nothing to fear but fear itself.

The caramel will last at least a week and can be used in an infinite number of ways: drizzled on pies, tarts and galettes, cheesecake, or on top of cookies, brownies, etc. Make a double batch and give the caramel sauce as a gift (see page 117). Look for a squeeze bottle (the kind diners use to serve ketchup) and you can have fun creating patterns and designs with the caramel.

INGREDIENTS

½ cup heavy cream

One 2-inch piece vanilla bean

1 cup sugar

3 tablespoons unsalted butter, at room temperature

1. Pour the cream into a small saucepan. Split the vanilla bean lengthwise with a small, sharp knife. Scrape the seeds into the cream, and add the empty bean. Bring the cream to a bare simmer over low heat, then remove from the heat and set aside.

2. Combine the sugar and 1 tablespoon of water in a small stainless-steel or ceramic saucepan. Bring to a boil. Swirl the pan occasionally to wash any burning sugar crystals off the sides of the pan, or use a pastry brush moistened with water to remove any sugar sticking to the sides of the pan. Cook until the mixture turns a golden caramel color. If you're using a candy thermometer,

bring to about 320 degrees F, being careful not to let it over-cook or burn.

3. Remove the sugar from the heat and immediately stir in the cream, being very careful since the sugar is very hot. (The mixture will bubble up a bit.) Whisk in the butter, stir-ring constantly, until it melts completely. Using a slotted spoon, carefully remove the vanilla bean.

4. Transfer the caramel to a squeeze bottle and use warm; store caramel at room temperature for a few hours, or refrigerate overnight. To reheat, fill a mixing bowl with the hottest tap water. Place the squeeze bottle in the bowl for 5 to 10 minutes, rotating occasionally, until the caramel loosens up. The caramel will keep for about 1 week.

SWEET PIE PASTRY

**MAKES ENOUGH DOUGH FOR
2 PIES, TARTS, GALETTES, OR
CROSTADAS**

This is a no-fail pastry for
pies, crostadas, and tarts;
it's perfect for those who
have a fear of making
homemade pie crust.
We use it to make the
Pecan Pie with Caramel
Sauce (page 128) and the
Caramel-Covered Apple
Galette (page 127). You can
make the pastry several
hours ahead of time and
refrigerate it until ready to
roll out and bake. You can
also freeze it for several
months, tightly wrapped
in foil.

INGREDIENTS

2 cups all-purpose flour

1½ tablespoons sugar

Pinch salt

1½ sticks (¾ cup) unsalted
butter, well chilled and cubed

¼ to ⅓ cup ice water

Place the flour, sugar, and
salt in the container of a food
processor and whirl several
times to mix. Add the butter,
coating it well with the flour,
and pulse about 15 times, or
until the butter resembles
coarse breadcrumbs. Add the
ice water slowly—a few tablespoons at a time—while whirl-
ing, until the dough starts to
adhere and pull away from the
sides of the food processor.
Wrap the dough in a large
sheet of foil and refrigerate for
at least 1 hour before rolling
out and baking.

CHOCOLATE-MINT CHRISTMAS CAKE

SERVES 10 TO 12

A cake just for the holidays! In this rich chocolate cake we use fresh mint instead of peppermint extract to infuse the cake with a fresh minty flavor. The cake is then garnished with crushed candy canes to give it a jewel-like finish. The cake can be baked and assembled up to 6 hours ahead of time, covered in the refrigerator, or lightly wrapped in foil and frozen for several months.

INGREDIENTS	
THE CAKE	**THE CHOCOLATE BUTTERCREAM**
2 sticks (1 cup) unsalted butter, cut into small pieces, plus more for greasing the pan	2 ounces chopped bittersweet chocolate (65% to 75% cacao)
8 ounces chopped bittersweet chocolate (65% to 75% cacao)	½ teaspoon water
1 teaspoon vanilla	¼ cup egg whites (from 2 large eggs)
¼ teaspoon salt	½ cup sugar
1½ cups sugar	1½ sticks (¾ cup) unsalted butter, at room temperature
¼ cup (loosely packed) fresh mint leaves, stems removed	: : : : :
6 large eggs, at room temperature	½ cup crushed candy canes or peppermint candies, for garnish (See Note)
¾ cup unsweetened cocoa powder	
¼ cup all-purpose flour	

1. *Prepare the cake:* Place a rack in the middle of the oven and preheat to 375 degrees F. Butter two 8-inch (round) cake pans. Line the bottoms of each pan with a round of wax paper or parchment paper cut to fit the pans, and butter the paper.

2. Melt the 2 sticks of butter and the 8 ounces of chocolate together in a double boiler (or in a metal bowl set over a pan of barely simmering water), stirring constantly. (We like to use the work bowl of our stand mixer as the top bowl of the double boiler, so there are fewer dishes to do.) Remove the pan from the heat as soon as the mixture is smooth, transfer to the work

Continued...

...*continued*

bowl of a standing mixer, and stir in the vanilla and salt.

3. Pulse the 1½ cups sugar and the mint together in a food processor until the mint is very finely chopped and pale green.

4. Add the mint sugar to the chocolate mixture and mix until smooth, about 1 minute on medium speed. With the machine on low, mix in the eggs one at a time, blending completely between additions. Sift the cocoa powder and flour over the batter and fold it in by hand until no dry spots remain. Divide the batter evenly between the two prepared pans and flatten the tops with a spatula.

5. Bake the cakes for 20 to 25 minutes, or until the tops of the cakes barely begin to crack. Let cool for about 5 minutes, then invert the cakes onto cooling racks and let cool completely.

6. *Meanwhile, make the buttercream:* Bring a medium pot of water to a simmer over low heat. Place the 2 ounces chocolate and ½ teaspoon water in another small saucepan set over very low heat and cook until the chocolate is melted and the mixture is smooth. Cool.

7. Place the egg whites and ½ cup sugar in the bowl of a standing mixer and place over the simmering water and whisk for about 2 minutes or until dissolved. Remove the bowl from the pot and place in the mixer. Using the whisk attachment whisk the egg whites and sugar for about 3 minutes, or until the mixture has cooled down. Remove the whisk attachment and place the paddle attachment onto the mixer. Working on medium speed, add the 1½ sticks butter one tablespoon at a time, whisking until smooth. Beat until the buttercream is smooth and thickened. Add the chocolate mixture and beat until smooth.

8. Spread 1 tablespoon of the frosting on the top of one cake, and place it top-side down on a cake platter. Spread a little less than half of the frosting onto this first cake, then place the second cake top-side up on the frosting. Use the remaining frosting to cover the rest of the cake. Sprinkle crushed candy canes around the perimeter of the cake, and chill until ready to serve, up to 24 hours ahead.

NOTE:
To crush the candy, place in a tightly sealed plastic bag and pound with a rolling pin, or place in a food processor and whirl until finely ground.

VARIATION:
If you are not a fan of fresh mint you can substitute 1 teaspoon vanilla or lemon extract in the cake batter.

STONEWALL KITCHEN
MENUS

Christmas Day

LOBSTER STEW WITH SAFFRON CREAM
(page 30)

**STANDING RIB ROAST STUDDED
WITH GARLIC** *(page 55)*

**SHARP CHEDDAR AND HERB
POPOVERS** *(page 107)*

FENNEL AND POTATO GRATIN *(page 90)*

**ORANGE-SCENTED MASHED BUTTERNUT
SQUASH** *(page 89)*

**SAUTÉED BRUSSELS SPROUTS WITH
NUTMEG-CARDAMOM CREAM AND
PANCETTA BREADCRUMBS** *(page 93)*

**CHOCOLATE-MINT CHRISTMAS
CAKE** *(page 133)*

ORANGE-GINGER SHORTBREAD *(page 122)*

First Night of Chanukah

**ROASTED ACORN SQUASH AND BEET
SALAD WITH MAPLE-RAISIN
VINAIGRETTE** *(page 19)*

**BRISKET WITH WINTER
VEGETABLES** *(page 59)*

**ALABASTER: MASHED POTATOES AND
TURNIPS** *(page 86) or* **POTATO PANCAKES**

**NOODLE KUGEL WITH RAISINS, APRICOTS,
AND SLIVERED ALMONDS** *(page 98)*

**POACHED PEARS WITH CHAMPAGNE-
GINGER-CINNAMON SYRUP** *(page 119)*

**CARAMEL-COVERED APPLE
GALETTE** *(page 127)*

Thanksgiving Feast

BUTTERNUT SQUASH SOUP WITH
CURRIED PECANS, APPLE, AND GOAT
CHEESE *(page 28)*

ROAST TURKEY WITH
CRANBERRY-PECAN STUFFING *(page 71)*

MASHED PARSNIPS AND PEARS *(page 87)*

SWEET WINTER SQUASH GRATIN *(page 92)*

ALABASTER: MASHED POTATOES
AND TURNIPS *(page 86)*

SAUTÉED BRUSSELS SPROUTS WITH
NUTMEG-CARDAMOM CREAM AND
PANCETTA BREADCRUMBS *(page 93)*

HOLIDAY ORANGE-CRANBERRY
SAUCE *(page 108)*

APPLE CIDER JELLY *(page 110)*

VANILLA BEAN CHEESECAKE WITH
CHOCOLATE CRUST *(page 124)*

PECAN PIE WITH CARAMEL SAUCE *(page 128)*

Holiday Open House Buffet

WINTER SPINACH SALAD WITH ROASTED
PEARS, BLUE CHEESE TOASTS, AND DRIED
CRANBERRY VINAIGRETTE *(page 22)*

CURRIED MAPLE PECANS *(page 49)*

HOPE'S SMOKED SALMON CRACKERS
WITH RED ONION–CAPER SAUCE *(page 37)*

INDIAN-SPICED MEATBALLS WITH
YOGURT AND MANGO CHUTNEY *(page 45)*

MINI LOBSTER CUPS *(page 40)*

HOLIDAY HAM WITH MAPLE SYRUP–
CLOVE-MARMALADE GLAZE *(page 77)*

APPLE CIDER JELLY *(page 110)*

ORANGE-GINGER SHORTBREAD *(page 122)*

ANDREA'S CHOCOLATE-DIPPED
BUTTERCRUNCH *(page 114)*

CHOCOLATE-MINT CHRISTMAS
CAKE *(page 133)*

New Year's Eve Cocktails

OYSTERS BAKED ON CREAMED
SPINACH WITH PARMESAN-PANKO CRUST
(page 33)

HOPE'S SMOKED SALMON CRACKERS
WITH RED ONION–CAPER SAUCE *(page 37)*

CURRIED MAPLE PECANS *(page 49)*

TARRAGON CRAB CANAPÉS *(page 39)*

INDIAN-SPICED MEATBALLS WITH
YOGURT AND MANGO CHUTNEY *(page 45)*

MINI LOBSTER CUPS *(page 40)*

CHAMPAGNE WITH FRESH-SQUEEZED
JUICES (POMEGRANATE, PASSION
FRUIT, ORANGE/GRAPEFRUIT)
AND COCKTAILS

Winter Night by the Fire

WINTER SPINACH SALAD WITH
ROASTED PEARS, BLUE CHEESE TOASTS,
AND DRIED CRANBERRY VINAIGRETTE
(page 22)

OSSO BUCO WITH ORANGE GREMOLATA
(page 67)

ORANGE-SCENTED MASHED BUTTERNUT
SQUASH *(page 89)*

THIN GREEN BEANS WITH BROWN
BUTTER AND ROASTED CHESTNUTS
(page 96)

POACHED PEARS WITH CHAMPAGNE-
GINGER-CINNAMON SYRUP *(page 119)*

I've-been-shopping-all-day-and-I'm-exhausted Dinner

BUTTERNUT SQUASH SOUP WITH
CURRIED PECANS, APPLE, AND
GOAT CHEESE *(page 28)*
(made ahead and just reheated)

WEDGE SALAD WITH BLUE CHEESE,
BACON, AND ROASTED SHALLOTS
(page 16)

ASSORTED BREADS

FOUR-BERRY CRISP *(page 120)*

Christmas Eve Get-together

LOBSTER STEW WITH SAFFRON CREAM
(page 30)

ROASTED ACORN SQUASH AND
BEET SALAD WITH MAPLE-RAISIN
VINAIGRETTE *(page 19)*

ROAST SALMON AND SCALLOPS WITH
ORANGE-CHAMPAGNE BEURRE
BLANC *(page 79)*

BAKED PASTA WITH ROASTED WILD
MUSHROOMS IN A CREAMY THYME
SAUCE *(page 81)*

THIN GREEN BEANS WITH BROWN BUTTER
AND ROASTED CHESTNUTS *(page 96)*

CARAMEL-COVERED APPLE
GALETTE *(page 127)*

VANILLA BEAN CHEESECAKE WITH
CHOCOLATE CRUST *(page 124)*

Winter Celebration: The First Real Snow

OYSTERS BAKED ON CREAMED SPINACH WITH PARMESAN-PANKO CRUST *(page 33)*

BEEF TENDERLOIN WITH HORSERADISH CRUST, ROASTED POTATOES, AND GARLIC *(page 53)*

ROASTED GARLIC, HERB, AND PARMESAN CUSTARD *(page 100)*

SWEET WINTER SQUASH GRATIN *(page 92)*

VANILLA BEAN CHEESECAKE WITH CHOCOLATE CRUST *(page 124)*

No More Rich Foods

BUTTERNUT SQUASH SOUP WITH CURRIED PECANS, APPLE, AND GOAT CHEESE *(page 28)*

WATERCRESS, TANGERINE, AND FENNEL SALAD WITH SPICE-ENCRUSTED TUNA *(page 25)*

POACHED PEARS WITH CHAMPAGNE-GINGER-CINNAMON SYRUP *(page 119)*

Thank Goodness It's All Over Supper

SIMPLEST PORK ROAST *(page 74)* *or* RACK OF LAMB WITH PISTACHIO-GARLIC-HERB CRUST AND ROASTED CHERRY TOMATOES *(page 65)*

APPLE CIDER JELLY *(page 110)*

FENNEL AND POTATO GRATIN *(page 90)*

MASHED PARSNIPS AND PEARS *(page 87)*

TOSSED GREEN SALAD

POACHED PEARS WITH CHAMPAGNE-GINGER-CINNAMON SYRUP *(page 119)*

INDEX

TABLE OF EQUIVALENTS

The exact equivalents in the following tables have been rounded for convenience.

LIQUID/DRY MEASUREMENTS	
U.S.	METRIC
¼ teaspoon	1.25 milliliters
½ teaspoon	2.5 milliliters
1 teaspoon	5 milliliters
1 tablespoon (3 teaspoons)	15 milliliters
1 fluid ounce (2 tablespoons)	30 milliliters
¼ cup	60 milliliters
⅓ cup	80 milliliters
½ cup	120 milliliters
1 cup	240 milliliters
1 pint (2 cups)	480 milliliters
1 quart (4 cups, 32 ounces)	960 milliliters
1 gallon (4 quarts)	3.84 liters
1 ounce (by weight)	28 grams
1 pound	448 grams
2.2 pounds	1 kilogram

LENGTHS	
U.S.	METRIC
⅛ inch	3 millimeters
¼ inch	6 millimeters
½ inch	12 millimeters
1 inch	2.5 centimeters

OVEN TEMPERATURE		
FAHRENHEIT	CELSIUS	GAS
250	120	½
275	140	1
300	150	2
325	160	3
350	180	4
375	190	5
400	200	6
425	220	7
450	230	8
475	240	9
500	260	10

Recipe *for* Disaster

Recipe
for Disaster

40 SUPERSTAR STORIES OF SUSTENANCE AND SURVIVAL

Alison Riley

CHRONICLE BOOKS
SAN FRANCISCO

Library of Congress Cataloging-in-
Publication Data available.

ISBN 978-1-7972-1282-1

Manufactured in China.

Design by Ben Wagner.
Typesetting by Sam Wagner.

Typeset in Minion Pro (Adobe Fonts,
Robert Slimbach), Victor Serif (Kometa),
and Mrs Eaves (Emigre, Zuzana Licko).

10 9 8 7 6 5 4 3 2 1

Chronicle books and gifts are
available at special quantity discounts
to corporations, professional
associations, literacy programs,
and other organizations. For details
and discount information, please
contact our premiums department at
corporatesales@chroniclebooks.com
or at 1-800-759-0190.

Chronicle Books LLC
680 Second Street
San Francisco, California 94107
www.chroniclebooks.com

For my dad, who I always thought was the author of the world's best hollandaise recipe, only to discover it came with our Cuisinart. Here's to you and me, and all the disasters behind us.

Contents

Introduction

While I am quite fluent in disasters, when it comes to cooking I am a person who needs a recipe. I do not possess the ability to throw things together to make a magical meal. Many of my friends and family members are alchemists of that kind, combining disparate ingredients from various cabinets in a way they just have a hunch might be complimentary. I have none of that. When I inquire about how somebody's chicken was prepared or a stew was created and they tell me to use a little turmeric, some shallots, throw in a chili pepper, or a bit of white wine, I know I am never going to make whatever they're describing. I need cold, hard measurements and instructions.

Though my creativity does not extend to the kitchen, much of my memory is punctuated by food. Pizelles my grandmother made at Christmas. My mother's baguettes that I loved and the ziti salad I never liked. Steak and cheese subs with my best friend in high school. Kimchi from care packages received by my college roommate. Oysters in Provincetown. Kofta in Marrakesh. Collards at home. While my wife was out of town for a long stretch, our son wrote a letter to her that was solely about how much he missed her tacos. Food is integral to our emotional lives, but while we plan, choose, and prepare special things when we revel and commemorate, on those days when there is less to celebrate, we still have to eat.

I embarked on this project with an idea of the humor and heartache it might yield, but hearing the stories people were generous enough to share brought the point of this project into real focus. This book is meant to remind us of the value of our experiences, both good and bad, and to bring levity and purpose to the moments we need them most. It was conceived through the deeply held belief that there is liberation and universal truth to be found through the exchange of *all* stories, even those full of sorrow, fear, or loneliness. From flat tires to pet deaths to unbearable losses, *Recipe for Disaster* aims to remember, without hierarchy or judgment, that our lowest moments offer something worth sharing: stories, food, and the welcome reminder that we've all been there.

In contemplating an example of my own, many stories came to mind. The first was a spectacularly catastrophic breakup, in the course of which there was fire and people died, and after which I was living alone in an apartment where I was used to sharing the rent. Between being sad, broke, and cooking illiterate, I made the same thing for dinner every night for months: steamed tofu and frozen spinach with sesame oil, tamari, and black sesame seeds alongside one slice of toast with Tofutti cream cheese. At the time,

I felt victorious as I prepared it because I was doing something for myself, not spending a lot of money, and not eating unhealthy things. I was comforted by the predictability and repetition of the ritual. It was like a meditation, or a quiet, daily promise to push forward and take care of myself. I know I stopped making this meal as the weather turned cold, about four or five months later, but I can't really say why. I don't think I was fully recovered from the heartbreak, but maybe I was sure I eventually would be.

A decade later, I contracted Lyme disease without knowing it and was not diagnosed until I was over a year into the infection. By then, I could barely move my arms and legs and could not buckle my own seat belt or button a shirt. I dressed myself in the evenings when I had slightly more mobility and then slept in my clothes, so I could use all my strength in the morning to dress my toddler for preschool. It was a wild and terrifying time. The infection eventually gave way to rheumatoid arthritis, and I adopted a strict anti-inflammatory diet to avoid the scariest medications and manage my symptoms. Eventually, my RA went into remission. This is a rather extreme version of a "recipe," but this was as low a point as I can recall, and food came to my rescue in a most literal way.

Many of the people who contributed to this book said that writing or talking with me about their stories was cathartic. Hearing them proved to be as well. I aspire to be like Ron Finley, who doesn't see memory as positive or negative. I can only hope to be as resilient as Laurie Woolever or as loyal to lost friends as Simon Doonan and Thundercat. I hope Samantha Irby's story gives us all permission to embrace what might feel embarrassing and offer it to others, rendering it powerless over any of us and empowering to us all. The responses to my question "Can you name a low point, of any size and shape, and the food memory you associate with surviving it?" are diverse in every way, but each of them feels unexpected and all of them comforting. People shared stories with me that they often had not otherwise shared at all. Beyond a map out of grief, beyond a collection of tales from interesting thinkers, that was the point: to surface what usually stays buried, however profound or pedestrian. To me, all of it is worth celebrating.

If nothing else, I hope this book proves that we are all dealt lemons. Collecting and sharing these stories is my version of lemonade.

—Alison Riley

Rejection Chicken by Samantha Irby

WRITER

1. First things first, you gotta get dumped. Everybody gets dumped! I have been broken up with dozens of times, mostly for reasons that I refuse to believe are my fault, and every single time the feeling I get afterward isn't sadness or despair or unrequited longing… it's hunger. I'm sure a more poetic person could come up with an analogy equating hunger and emotional emptiness or something, but I don't talk like that. I eat my feelings. I have a lot of feelings, and I eat them, especially when the feeling in question is LIKE PURE SHIT. So you've been rejected, you're some gross combination of mad and/or sad about it, but you still need to eat. Go to the store to get ice cream and also grab:

   INGREDIENTS

   1 pack of chicken thighs (get a pound?)

   Ground cinnamon

   Curry powder

   Olive oil

   1 yellow onion

   4 zucchini

   Pepper and the dehydrated salt from your tears

   2 cups [480 ml] of cream

   One 32 oz [960 ml] box of chicken broth

   Jasmine rice or leftover take-out rice or whatever rice-adjacent foodstuff you enjoy

   Fresh basil (if you are fancy)

   A pack of slivered almonds

2. Okay, now that we're ready to cook, the first thing you have to do is put on your sad playlist. I make very specific playlists for myself, and the theme of 95 percent of them is "cool funeral." I'd recommend blasting the saddest songs you can think of from a speaker, but before I got one, I would just throw my phone in a coffee cup to amplify the sound, and you know what? That's fine, who cares! Pairing a Bluetooth on shitty Wi-Fi is torture, so skip it.

3. Cut the chicken into chunks and put them in a large bowl. Cutting up slimy dead meat is a yucky feeling that I ordinarily avoid, but I *promise* having to saw through those weird fatty white strings and the occasional bloody piece with your dull, regular-person knives is worth it, or, at the very least, will distract you from your malaise for at least a few minutes. If you're really goth,

cont.

you can pretend it's one of your ex's tender vital organs. Once it's all cut up, uncap both your cinnamon and your curry powder and liberally shake them over the chicken. Stir the pieces or flip them over using whatever tool feels practical to you to coat them evenly, then set the bowl aside.

4. Put your cast-iron Dutch oven on the stovetop, turn the heat on low, and put a couple glugs of olive oil in the pan. A thing you need to know about me is that I have no idea what differentiates good olive oil from bad, and I have absolutely zero interest in learning. This is a meal you are going to eat on the toilet while you weep, so it truly does not matter if your olive oil came from the garbage. Okay, so you're heating your pan and your oil on the lowest heat setting, and while that magic happens you're going to slice your onion however you like onions to be sliced, and drop them in the pan. As they start sizzling, wash your zucchini, cut the ends off, then I like to slice them on a severe angle because it looks cool and chef-y, but honestly? It doesn't matter! Does anything?????? Once the zucchini are sliced up, drop them in the pan with the onion and the hot oil, stir to coat, and turn the heat up a touch.

5. Are you feeling like a cook now? This is the part where I look around the kitchen, thrilled by the sounds and the smells and low-key in awe that I am the one making those things happen, and break my fucking arm trying to pat myself on the back. But we're not done! Season the zucchini and onions with lots of salt and pepper as they cook, and as things start to soften a bit, dump in your chicken chunks and another glug of olive oil if shit is looking dry. Stir everything again and don't worry—the cinnamon/curry mixture might look a little muddy, but trust me, it's fine.

6. Now is a good time, while the chicken cooks, to unfollow your ex on social media and block their phone number. I mean, unless they need to coordinate picking up the bike they left in your front hall or whatever, why would you need to hear from them? Keep an eye on the pan as you drop their follower count from seventy-four to seventy-three, and when the chicken gets kinda bouncy (I am not sure which adjective I should use instead of this one, so hopefully it's clear what I mean) and cooked-looking, pour the entire pint of cream into the pan.

7. Technically, you could stop here. You could heat the cream through and season it to taste and just be done with it. And if that's where you're at? I respect it. I like to make it slightly less rich—i.e., add some mildly flavored water to it so that it makes more sauce and I can stretch it over a couple of days. So, I pour in an entire box of broth and bring it to a slow boil, then let it simmer for a little while so the flavors can meld. And while that alchemy is happening, I make a pot of rice, and I will not insult you by assuming you don't know how to do that.

8. When your rice is done and your rejection chicken (sad person curry!) is hot, season to taste with salt and pepper, then sprinkle some basil on it and throw handfuls of slivered almonds in it, serve it over scoops of hot rice in the biggest bowl you feel comfortable crawling into bed with, and eat and eat and eat until that deep well of sadness inside you is filled with chicken and nuts and cream. Then, delete all of your cutie little text threads and throw out the old anniversary cards and wash your face and go to bed. And there will still be some left when you wake up starving and sobbing over that moron (I know, I get it) tomorrow.

In Bed with No Fever by Sarah Silverman

COMEDIAN

I was thirteen the first time I experienced long-term clinical depression. It came over me as fast as a cloud covers the sun. As fast as when you are fine one moment and the next you're like, "Oh fuck, I have the flu." It was my first experience with depression, my first experience with having monumental, cellular-level change that happens in an instant. There was no cinematic slow motion telling me, "This is big." No music tipping me off to trauma. It just...happened. And suddenly, my perspective had shifted—maybe just one single degree, but the whole world looked different.

I went from being a social butterfly to not wanting to be with or talk to anyone. Not even my identical twin best friend. I loved school, and now I couldn't bear to go. I missed three straight months of school for reasons I couldn't articulate. I stayed in a ball in bed with no fever, no cough, no physicalization of un-wellness.

And just one sensory joy. Pinwheels. Chocolate-covered marshmallow cookies. When I see them at the grocery store now, they make me so sad for that little New Hampshire kid who didn't know what was wrong with her. But they were my salvation.

Under the Sea by Hannah Black and Carla Perez-Gallardo

FOUNDING PARTNERS OF LIL DEB'S OASIS

Our restaurant has a vibey, buzzy energy on a regular night, but for New Year's Eve, we like to take it to the next level. There is always a theme that involves costumes, decor, a playlist, *and* a complex multicourse dinner menu that is conceptually aligned. We are ambitious, to say the least. Every December 31, over the course of our three seatings, there is a very hard and fast learning curve as we figure out these new dishes and service styles in real time, in front of our live audience of paying customers.

Our third annual New Year's Eve party, *Under the Sea*, stands out the most. Naturally, we crafted a seafood-focused multicourse meal, and our staff were all dressed as sea creatures, mermaids, and divers. Green and blue crepe streamers were hanging from the ceiling as waves and algae. The first turn was rough; there were a lot of kinks to work out. We had ambitiously put a squid-ink paella on the menu as our main course and had not had a lot of time to test the timing, so the food wasn't coming out as fast as it should. The 6 p.m. block of NYE diners is always a little awkward—it's just too early. But we made it through more or less on time, and the people left happy.

Now time for the second turn. We were ready, kinks ironed out, *bring it on!* As our first customers for the 8 p.m. seating sat down, we felt confident that we had everything under control. The lights were dim, the kitchen was humming, and the music was bumping. Until . . . *drip, drip*, our lead line cook felt a few droplets of an unidentified liquid on their head. *Drip, drip*. "What the fuck is that!?" we thought in sheer panic, quickly assuring the customers sitting in direct view that there was not a bathroom directly above. We darted upstairs, to our private dining room, where some of our staff had been setting up the illegal bar for our overflow. There was our culprit. A boxed wine, a silver bladder containing the equivalent of three bottles, had accidentally burst and there was organic tempranillo flowing everywhere and dripping down through the floorboards. Could be worse.

We joked with our customers that here at Lil' Deb's Oasis it rains wine, cleaned up the mess, and proceeded to move on with the 8 p.m. seating, applying what we learned in the first turn to ensure a smoother service.

Finally it's time, the 10 p.m. seating, the most special of them all! We rush to clean and reset the tables of the previous guests, knowing that we are running a little behind. The goal is to get the desserts out before midnight, and we are racing against the clock. We have confidence that this will be the smoothest and most fun of the three seatings—after all, the real fun begins after the clock strikes midnight. But nay. Reports start coming back from our servers: One table is saying that they are full after the first course, another table is barely eating, another table is just a bit odd. Everyone seemed to be thoroughly enjoying themselves, no one seemed particularly perturbed, no food was sent back, but the kitchen was frustrated. We finally had it! This was gonna be good! Why was nobody eating? Slowly it dawned on us: Nearly half the restaurant was tripping on mushrooms (usually the 10 p.m. seating is full of our friends, so that checks out). Everyone was just really, really high. Too high to eat our delicious, lovingly prepared meal.

Eventually midnight rolled around, and dessert had not yet been sent out. We got into our positions anyway, mounting the bar to release the celebratory confetti cannons. "5, 4, 3, 2, 1, HAPPY NEW YEAR!!!!!" All the fish and mermaids, lobsters and deep sea divers hugged and kissed each other, many of them deep in the trenches of a psychedelic journey. We went around and offered dessert to anyone who wanted it, but there was no going back—the party had begun, and tables were cleared to make room for the dance floor. It was a brand-new year.

This year was a particularly new dawn, as it was the last service before a major renovation project began in our space. We had been grinding it out for the previous three years in an incredibly small and dysfunctional space. This was our final hurrah, our goodbye to the old and a welcoming into our glow-up. We partied hard that night, crepe paper confetti mixing with squid ink rice, sticking to the bottom of our platform heels. A group of close friends gathered in our kitchen, a space that we lovingly referred to as a "shithole" (there was a literal hole in the floor, so . . .), to pay our respects to the past and say our goodbyes. We laughed and cried in near disbelief at how far we had come. Eventually, a particularly drunk and expressive gesture was followed by a large crash. Three entire racks of freshly

Nearly half
the restaurant
was tripping
on mushrooms.

washed glasses, stacked precariously on the edge of a lowboy, had fallen to the floor. Glass shards everywhere, the floor beyond filthy. That was a sign: It was time to go. We closed up shop, and the next week, the entire kitchen was demolished.

It was three long months until we were able to reopen. As the saying goes, construction always takes twice as long and is twice as expensive as you'd expect. We were cleaning up dried squid ink rice until the day we reopened. It really gets everywhere.

Squid Ink Paella

INGREDIENTS (FOR 4—6)

For the shellfish

1 lb [455 g] cockles or clams

8 oz [230 g] mussels

1 cup [240 ml] white wine

4 garlic cloves, whole

2 tsp red pepper flakes

For the mushroom stock

4 cups [150 g] dried shiitakes

8 cups [2 L] water

For the rice

1 cup [200 g] Arborio rice

2 Tbsp extra-virgin olive oil

1 medium onion, finely chopped

6 garlic cloves, minced

1 tsp smoked paprika

1 tsp salt

To finish

2 tsp squid or cuttlefish ink

2 scallions, finely chopped

2 Tbsp unsalted butter

1 in [2.5 cm] piece ginger, peeled and finely grated

METHOD OF PREPARATION

1. *To prepare the shellfish:* Clean the shellfish under cold water. Scrub off any residue and set aside in separate bowls.

2. *To make the mushroom stock:* In a medium saucepan, cover the mushrooms with the water and bring to a boil over high heat. Lower the heat and simmer for 30 minutes. Strain and reserve the liquid—you should have about 4 cups [1 L] of stock. Reserve 1 cup [250 ml] of the mushrooms, slice into thin pieces, and set aside.

3. While the mushroom stock is simmering, make the rice: Toast the rice in a heavy-bottomed pan over medium heat until fragrant, stirring frequently with a wooden spoon, 4 to 6 minutes. Get a tiny bit of color on it, but nothing too toasty or the grains will dry out. Transfer to a bowl and set aside.

4. *To cook the shellfish:* In a medium pot with a tight-fitting lid, bring wine, garlic, and red pepper flakes to a boil. Once bubbling, drop the cockles in and cover until they begin to open, about 2 minutes. Quickly remove with a slotted spoon and set aside. Repeat with the mussels. Strain the liquid through a fine-mesh strainer to remove any sand or silt and set aside.

5. *To cook the rice:* In the heavy-bottomed pot used to toast the rice, add the olive oil and onion and sauté over medium heat until translucent, about 5 minutes. Add the garlic, smoked paprika, and salt and sauté another 3 minutes or so. Add the rice back to the pot and stir to combine. Add the reserved wine/shellfish liquid, stirring constantly with a wooden spoon until the liquid is absorbed into the rice. Stirring will help release the starches, making the rice creamy and delicious.

6. Add the reserved mushroom stock, 1 cup [250 ml] at a time, to the rice and onion mixture, stirring constantly. Each time the liquid is absorbed into the rice, add another cup of stock and continue stirring. Repeat until at least 3 cups [750 ml] of the stock have been used. Taste the rice, which should be soft and creamy but slightly al dente on the inside. If it needs a bit more liquid, add a little at a time. This whole process will take about 20 minutes.

7. *To finish the rice:* A few minutes before the rice is ready, throw in the squid ink, scallions, butter, and ginger. Stir briskly until the ink has fully incorporated, then place the opened shellfish over the rice. Reduce the heat to the lowest setting and cover. Allow to steam for 2 to 3 minutes.

8. Serve immediately and enjoy, ideally with a glass of tempranillo and a salad of your choice.

Seasoned, Not Sauced by Bowen Yang

ACTOR, COMEDIAN

I am one of those weird people who doesn't like their mapo tofu stewy, or moist, or swimming in sauce. I don't appreciate the colloidal properties of what a generally imagined mapo tofu would be. My mother is, um, only a moderately skilled cook. She wasn't really one for domesticity, but she did her best. I took it out on her a little too often as a child, telling her directly how much I didn't enjoy her cooking, which fills me with a lot of guilt and shame now.

She would always make, and still makes, her mapo tofu extremely dry, which has somehow made me acquire the taste for dry mapo tofu. I like it with a firm tofu, and I like it seasoned and not sauced, though there's still a layer of sauce and obviously the tofu absorbs the peppercorn and the doubanjiang. It absorbs all those flavors and complements the minced pork that tradition calls for. It's very dry and sits perfectly on a bed of white rice. But it's one of the "mistakes" that has made me appreciate my mother's cooking now because it is what I am used to, and I realize that she has been able to pass down this weird anomaly to my palate, which informs what I like eating nowadays.

It's the first thing I ask her to make when I go home to Colorado, where she lives with my dad. It is just about the most comforting food that someone else can make for me. I can only hope that my love for her specific, errant, incorrect kind of mapo tofu makes up for all the years that I was not so gracious and kind about her cooking.

ODDBALL by Michael W. Twitty

AUTHOR, CULINARY HISTORIAN

My mother was making a pot of soup. It had beans in it, and at the time, I didn't like beans. Fifteen beans to be exact, an onion, and a ham bone saved over from the holiday. It matters that I didn't want any and wouldn't eat with her. We had nothing to share. I was just watching her make the soup, with a scowl.

I was tense, but she was tenser. A year before, I had come out at sixteen years old—I don't remember how, but I asserted myself. And every Saturday after that I would go to SMYAL, the Sexual Minority Youth Assistant League, DC's LGBTQ youth group then located in an upstairs loft in Capitol Hill, not far from the Library of Congress. There was nothing drastic about my journey. I mean, I did come out in my school newspaper and I wanted to be seen, but more than that I wanted to be loved for who I had always known myself to be.

She kept stirring. I think the stirring was passive-aggressive, but I don't know that for a fact; we are an often nonverbal culture where gestures are encyclopedias of emotion. My lips wanted to move but they didn't. I kept starting to breathe, then stopping, massaging all the hesitation on my teeth and through my nose. The soup smelled good, but I still didn't want any. I had no hunger, but then I pushed it out:

"There's this community forum in the city next week. I volunteered to speak, can I go?"

"A community forum on what?" My mother stopped stirring.

"On gay rights and gay teens."

"No, I don't think that's a good idea. You can't go."

For the first time in a long time, my mother said I couldn't go anywhere or do something.

"But, Mom, I volunteered and I will be safe riding the Metro—"

"Michael, you are MY child and I said NO!" The wooden spoon almost broke as she tapped it on the edge of the big pot. "Why . . . why do you always have to be the FUCKING ODDBALL of the family?"

"I . . . ummm . . . don't . . . "

I had no answer for her. Oddball? Fucking oddball? This was news to me. I thought until that moment that it was okay to be myself. I didn't know that I was the different one, the odd one, the stranger in our own gates. I was heartbroken and I wanted to die. I've heard those words every single day of my life since.

It wasn't until my mom passed almost twenty years later that I revisited that moment. I really wasn't the oddball of the family; the family was full of oddballs, and that's what made her so mad other than the fact that she was trying to protect me from my own vulnerabilities and was failing miserably. My mother wanted normalcy; she had Black Ozzie and Harriet fantasies, and as time moved on, our family's inherent dysfunction drifted her further and further away from the dream to be, as she once put it, "garden-variety African Americans."

This was the same woman who sat me down and gave me the Van Gogh talk. She explained that his brother Theo tried to encourage Vincent out of his depression by exhorting him to value and invest in his happiness and self-esteem. She read me his letters. I had to make myself happy and find joy in my truth. But I was her oddball.

Unless it meant being gay. Mom didn't mean the harm she caused and I never brought it up. One day she said randomly, "I'm sorry for anything I've said or done that hurt you." It hurt too much to unbury the words, but my mother's love was unquestioned—faults and all. And yet, I'm pretty sure if I ever got a tattoo—and I won't—it would say "oddball."

Without a Gathering, a Good Salad
by Alice Waters

AUTHOR, CHEF, FOOD ACTIVIST

I'm sure many people feel this way, but I can say with certainty that I've never lived through any period more professionally and personally challenging than the pandemic. I've witnessed many passages of cultural upheaval: the Vietnam War, Women's Liberation, the Civil Rights Movement, the AIDS crisis (to name just a handful). But there's something about this time that I've found to be especially devastating. I opened my restaurant, Chez Panisse, in 1971 with a bunch of close friends. We wanted it to be a place where people could gather and eat together; a place for the community, but also a refuge for activists, fomenters, and anyone who had been marginalized by mainstream American society. We were Berkeley hippies who had radical ideas about how we wanted to live, talk, create, love, and share. At its core, Chez Panisse was built on these mutually held values. At the beginning of the pandemic, I was reminded of the early days of AIDS, when no one really understood what we were facing—not scientifically, but not culturally either. AIDS patients became pariahs. People I knew and loved were getting sick, and few places felt safe from persecution and scrutiny. I was determined to keep the restaurant open to all, for it to be a haven, even as many were being overcome by fear.

Back in February of 2020, I thought coronavirus might be similar. We've been open for nearly fifty years—we've seen disasters, overcome obstacles. I imagined Chez Panisse might once again be the gathering place it has been during periods of turmoil. But, of course, we quickly learned that gathering was in fact precisely what we should not do. We decided to close the restaurant. It was one of the hardest moments of my life.

I live by myself and am completely dependent on the restaurant for my social world. It's not just a place to bring my friends to dinner, or feed the people I love; the restaurant itself is my companion. And I wasn't just worried about myself, of course; I was worried about the more than one hundred employees who make up what I call "La Famille Panisse." How could I continue to take care of them? How could I take care of the farmers who depended on us for their survival? We very quickly figured out how to offer our customers the pristine produce we once

prepared for them directly in the form of farm boxes, and then slowly built up to a take-out business. Through all of this change, the agony of uncertainty, and the real, genuine loneliness of this time, I've looked forward to the beautiful boxes of salad greens delivered to me from the restaurant. Each day, opening my box of perfect greens from my friend Bob Cannard and his son Ross's farm—sometimes blushing pink chicories like rose petals, with slices of grapefruit. Sometimes spicy arugula with salty toasted hazelnuts and ricotta salata. A good salad will buoy my spirits. A good salad—I now realize—will help see me through calamity.

This is a recipe for our classic Chez Panisse vinaigrette. It is the sauce I make most often, and if it's made out of good olive oil and good wine vinegar, it's the best salad dressing I can imagine. At its simplest, vinaigrette is a mixture of vinegar and oil in a ratio of one part vinegar to about three or four parts oil. Start by estimating roughly how much vinaigrette you will need. This depends on what you're using it for; a quarter cup is more than enough for four servings of green salad, for example, but you really never need to measure out exact amounts. Start by pouring the vinegar into a bowl. Dissolve a pinch of salt in it and taste for balance. The salt has a real relationship with the vinegar. When you add just enough salt, it subdues the acid of the vinegar and brings it into a wonderful balance. Try adding salt bit by bit and tasting to see what happens. How much salt is too much? How much is too little? What tastes best? If you add too much salt, just add a touch more vinegar.

Grind in some black pepper and whisk in the oil. The vinaigrette should taste brightly balanced, neither too oily nor overly acidic. Adjust the sauce, adding more vinegar if you've added too much oil, and more salt, if it needs it.

Classic Chez Panisse Vinaigrette

INGREDIENTS (FOR 4)

1 Tbsp red wine vinegar

Salt and freshly ground black pepper

3 to 4 Tbsp [45 to 60 ml] extra-virgin olive oil

METHOD OF PREPARATION

1. Pour the red wine vinegar into a small bowl.

2. Add salt and black pepper. Stir to dissolve the salt. Adjust to taste.

3. With a fork or a small whisk, beat in the extra-virgin olive oil a little at a time.

4. Taste as you go and stop when it tastes right.

VARIATIONS

- Add a little puréed garlic or diced shallot, or both, to the vinegar.

- White wine vinegar, sherry vinegar, or lemon juice can replace some or all of the red wine vinegar.

- Beat in a little mustard before you start adding the oil.

- For part of the olive oil, substitute a very fresh nut oil, such as walnut or hazelnut.

- Heavy cream or crème fraîche can replace some or all of the olive oil.

- Chop some fresh herbs and stir them into the finished vinaigrette.

The Best of the Worst by Laurie Woolever

WRITER, EDITOR

A few years ago, in late spring, my unhappy marriage imploded, messily and inevitably, one terrible Monday night. It was both a massive relief and a terrifying tectonic shift. I started sleeping on the couch. The next morning, I made an emergency call to my longtime therapist, but she couldn't really talk for long, she said, because her husband had just died unexpectedly, violently, and the police were still in her home. I turned to the nonprofessional advice of others.

My boss, Tony Bourdain, who was a mentor to me and many others, a generous, charismatic, mysterious, and brilliant person around whom many universes were centered, was reassuring when I told him that I was getting divorced and looking for a new home. He'd been through it, too.

"It's gonna suck, a lot, at first," he said. "But then you're gonna realize how much better off you are. Don't get a shitty apartment because you think you can't afford something better," he said. "Whatever you need, I will help you." I got myself a good apartment, secure in the knowledge that he would have my back.

A month later, he took his own life.

I was subsisting on Hi-Chew candy and nicotine gum, too unmoored and anxious to eat normally. On the day that the news of Tony's death broke, a cruelly bright and perfect summer Friday, my friend Alison invited me into her cool, shaded kitchen, handed me a can of seltzer, and made me a bowl of soft scrambled eggs, the best thing I'd eaten, or would eat, that summer.

Soft Scrambled Eggs

4 eggs

2 Tbsp butter

Salt and pepper

METHOD OF PREPARATION

1. Crack the eggs into a bowl and gently whip them with a fork to break the yolks and mostly incorporate the yolks and whites. If you really want soft and creamy scrambled eggs, you shouldn't go crazy here; whisking vigorously incorporates more air, which makes for firmer, drier scrambled eggs.

2. In a medium skillet, preferably nonstick, heat the butter over medium heat until it forms tiny foamy bubbles that then subside.

3. Reduce the heat to medium-low, pour the eggs into the pan, and swirl them around a bit. Use a wooden spoon or rubber or silicone spatula to gently and more or less continuously move the eggs around as they cook, in a loose figure-eight pattern, making sure to hit all parts of the pan, releasing steam and keeping the eggs from cooking too quickly.

4. As soon as the eggs are cooked through but still soft, which should only take a few minutes, remove the pan from the heat, season the eggs with as much salt and pepper as you like, divide them between two shallow bowls, and serve immediately, with buttered toast or whatever else appeals.

It's gonna suck, a lot, at first. But then you're gonna realize how much better off you are.

Portrait of a Single Father by Cey Adams

ARTIST

My only son, Eric, was born in the winter of 1984. I remember thinking I was not prepared to be a twenty-year-old dad. I was completely scared and unsure that I had any real-life parenting skills. My older sister, sensing I was looking for moral support, sat me down at the kitchen table with a bowl of our mom's warm bread pudding, and reminded me of my responsibilities as his father. After I finished eating and listening, I felt calm enough to make some decisions about my future. I decided to put my teenage graffiti-writing shenanigans behind me and become a man. I grabbed a piece of paper, made a list of business contacts and anyone I felt could help move my art career forward, and officially set up shop as a professional artist and graphic designer. I did anything—from gallery exhibitions, murals, and commissioned pieces to logo designs and advertising campaigns for corporate brands. I quickly learned that being an independent, small business owner meant doing everything on my own. Up to this point, the difficulties working parents faced from day to day had never occurred to me. But as a single father in New York City, bringing my son to work sites and meetings became a normal routine.

In the early 1980s, it was beyond uncommon to see a young dad like myself changing a dirty diaper in a public space. I remember one time we were headed to DC by train to visit family. As we sat in the lounge area waiting to board, I suddenly smelled something sour coming from my baby's onesie. I knew this was going to get messy real quick! Imagine me running around Penn Station, two bags over my shoulder, holding my son and looking for a restroom. Looking back, it felt like a scene in a movie. There I was running around the city holding a bomb that was about to explode!

I located the nearest restroom and dashed inside. Not only was there no changing station or table, but the place was filthy and smelly. The floor was a wet, slippery combination of footprints, mud, and urine from guys peeing anywhere and everywhere. Yuck!! I looked down at my little boy's sweet face and knew what I had to do. Without hesitation, I took off my jacket, laid it down on the nasty floor, and changed his dirty diaper. I felt a strange joy come over me. I was proud to be a father!

Once we were comfortable and settled on the train, I thought: Everything is going to be okay. I thought about my life and my son's life. I imagined the aroma of my mom's warm bread pudding again . . . Calm set in. Eric closed his eyes, I closed mine, and we both drifted off to sleep.

Bread Pudding

INGREDIENTS (FOR 4)

For the bread pudding

1 cup [140 ml] raisins

¼ cup [60 ml] Kentucky bourbon

1 loaf French bread, at least a day old

4 cups [960 ml] milk

3 large eggs

2 cups [400 g] sugar

2 Tbsp vanilla extract

¼ tsp allspice

½ tsp ground cinnamon

3 Tbsp butter, melted

For the bourbon sauce

½ cup [110 g] butter

1 cup [200 g] sugar

1 large egg

½ cup [120 ml] Kentucky bourbon [less or more to taste]

METHOD OF PREPARATION

1. *To make the bread pudding:* In a small bowl, combine the raisins and bourbon. Cover and soak for 1 to 2 hours.

2. Preheat the oven to 350°F (180°C).

3. Cut the bread into 1 in [2.5 cm] cubes.

4. Place the milk in a large mixing bowl and add the bread. Press the bread into the milk until all milk is absorbed.

5. In a separate bowl, whisk the eggs, then add the sugar, vanilla, allspice, and cinnamon and whisk together. Pour over the bread and milk mixture.

6. Add the bourbon-soaked raisins (with or without the remaining soaking liquid, according to taste). Stir gently to combine.

7. Pour the melted butter into the bottom of a 9 by 13 in [23 by 33 cm] baking pan, coating the bottom and sides. Pour the bread, milk, and egg mixture into the baking pan.

8. Bake for 35 to 45 minutes, until the liquid is set. The pudding is done when the edges brown and pull away from the sides of the pan. This can also be made in individual ramekins.

9. *While the bread pudding is baking, make the sauce:* Melt the butter in a medium saucepan over low heat. Add the sugar and egg and whisk to blend well.

10. Slowly cook over low heat, stirring constantly, until the mixture thickens enough to coat the back of a spoon, then remove from the heat. Do not allow the mixture to simmer, or the sauce will curdle. If the sauce curdles, take it off the heat and blend it smooth in a blender.

11. Whisk in the bourbon to taste. Whisk again before serving. The sauce should be soft, creamy, and smooth.

12. Serve the bread pudding with the bourbon sauce on the side.

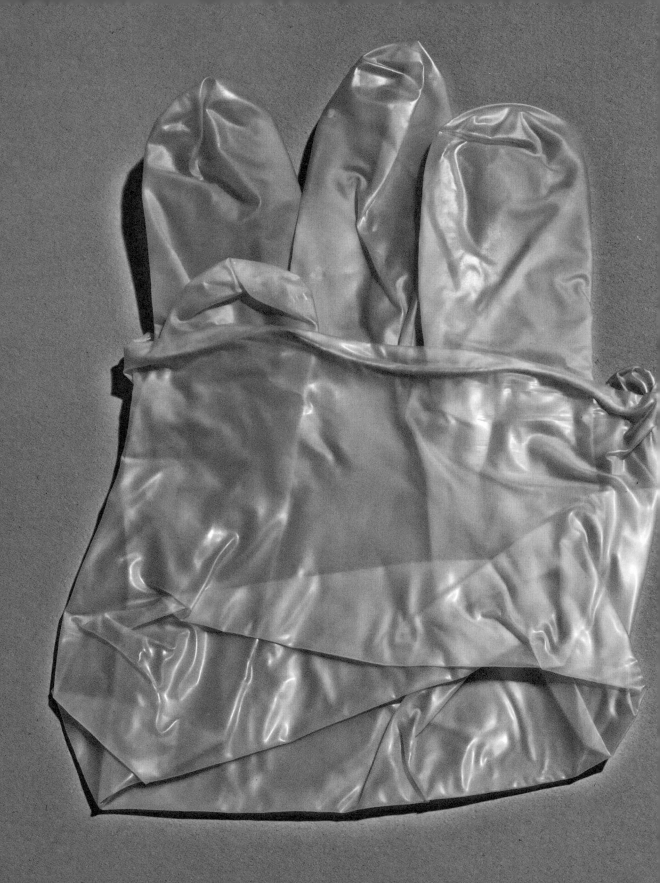

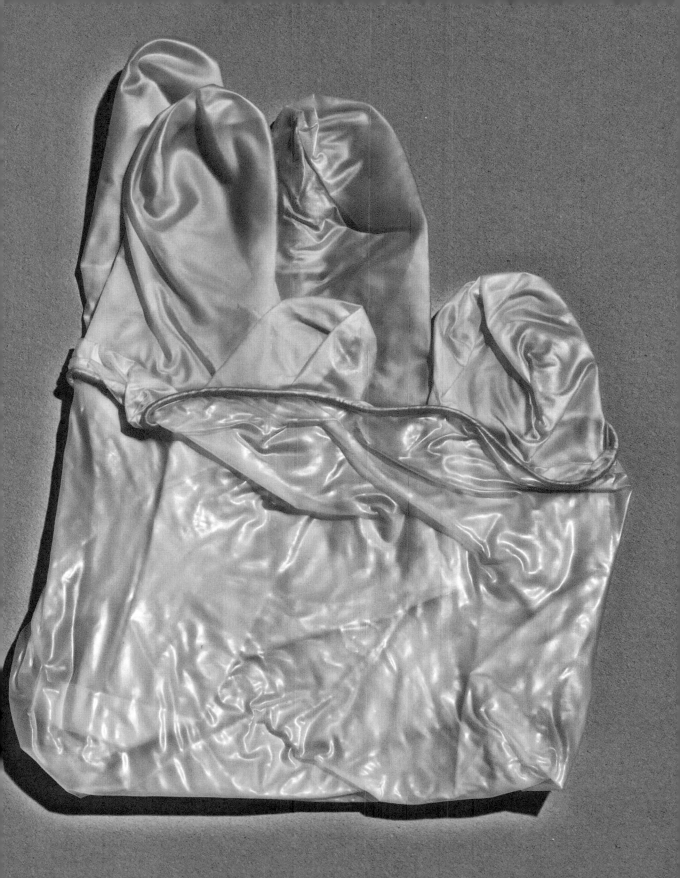

Pesto to Pass Time by Chelsea Peretti

ACTOR, WRITER, COMEDIAN

Chelsea Peretti: You know what I made a ton of in the pandemic is pesto. Pesto with tons of garlic, and then I put lemon zest in it. I put it in my mini Cuisinart, and everything about it is so zippy.

Alison Riley: Right, it's refreshing.

CP: It's like also kind of a depression food cause it cuts through—the basil, the garlic, the lemon—and if you don't respond to one of those with some part of your body, then you are in a truly dark place.

AR: Do you make it and freeze it or do you just make it per meal?

CP: No, my mom is all about freezing things all the time . . . She's like, "Actually, you can put it in ice cube trays . . ." but I don't like defrosting. I feel like defrosting is a whole science. What's appealing about pesto is the freshness of it and the vitality of it, and it's so easy to make. I don't feel the need to freeze for the future.

AR: And cooking passes pandemic time.

CP: Yes, it was a good pandemic malaise recipe because part of the pandemic was living out the same day over and over and trying to find ways to keep yourself stimulated and excited to be alive. Turns out, that's pesto.

Basil Pesto

Disclaimer: Italian traditionalists, please be aware this is some California-style improvisation. Please don't be mad at me!

INGREDIENTS (FOR 2)

1 cup [240 ml] extra-virgin olive oil

1 lemon

½ cup [60 g] pine nuts

¾ cup [25 g] grated Parmesan

2 cups [25 g] basil leaves

1 to 3 garlic cloves, peeled

Salt

METHOD OF PREPARATION

1. Fill the bottom of a mini food processor with olive oil to about ½ in [1.3 cm] high.

2. Slice or zest (yellow skin only) half of a lemon and add that to the food processor.

3. In a small skillet, brown the pine nuts, adding a handful or more to taste (or budget). I'm sure some other nut could work in a pinch. Add them to the food processor.

4. Add the Parmesan.

5. Add two handfuls of basil leaves (I include buds but remove stems).

6. Add the garlic depending on how depressed you are.

7. Add salt (or truffle salt!) to taste.

8. Blend until a paste forms. Add more olive oil to loosen. Taste and add more of anything that is missing.

If you don't respond to one of those with some part of your body, then you are in a truly dark place.

A Balm Then, a Balm Now by Tien Nguyen

WRITER

When I was about thirteen, my mother started working two, three jobs a week, pulling a double or triple most days. This meant she usually left very early and returned home very late. My sisters and I made do with microwavable dinners, Kraft Mac and Cheese, sandwiches. Sometimes, though, my mom got home early enough and rustled up what she named trứng flat ("flat eggs"): eggs beaten with fish sauce, pepper, and chopped scallions, cooked like a giant omelet, and eaten with steamed rice. It took all of five minutes to throw together. Combining fish sauce with eggs is so common in Vietnamese households that I'm sure others grew up eating some version of this, too. Still, for us, trứng flat was a real treat and fed us through some miserable times.

Not too long ago, I learned of a homey northern Vietnamese dish called chả trứng chiên. Most variations involve beating eggs with fish sauce, pepper, and scallions before adding seasoned ground chicken or pork to the mix. If you're flush, crab or mussels aren't out of place, either. The point is, meat is a very common ingredient—and that meat is the difference between a trứng flat and a chả trứng chiên. I've realized, belatedly, that had she not been short on two things (time, money), my mom might have made chả trứng chiên instead of trứng flat. It's hard for me not to think of trứng flat now as a dish of both survival and omission. Still, I have a right fondness for it. I make it when I'm blue, or when I need a quick meal. It was a balm then. It is a balm now.

It's hard for me
not to think of
trứng flat now
as a dish of
both survival
and omission.

Trứng Flat (Flat Eggs)

I use an 8 in [20 cm] nonstick pan for this, but you can use any pan you have on hand, though a larger pan will result in a flatter trứng flat (as the eggs will spread more), and, conversely, a smaller pan will yield a thicker one. This recipe can easily be scaled up as needed, and leftovers can be transferred to an airtight container and refrigerated for up to 3 days.

INGREDIENTS (FOR 2)

3 large eggs

2 to 3 scallions, white and green parts, sliced, plus more for serving

1 tsp fish sauce, plus more for serving

Freshly ground black pepper

1 Tbsp unsalted butter

Steamed rice, for serving

Furikake, for serving

METHOD OF PREPARATION

1. Crack the eggs into a large bowl and add the scallions, fish sauce, and a pinch of black pepper. Beat well to combine.

2. In an 8 in [20 cm] pan set over medium-low heat, melt the butter. When it begins to froth, pour in the eggs. Cook, undisturbed, until the eggs are set, just a few minutes. Then, using a spatula, divide the eggs in half. Carefully flip each half over and cook until that side has set, 30 seconds to 1 minute. Slide the eggs onto a serving plate and cut into squares or wedges.

3. To serve, scoop steamed rice into a bowl. Place the trứng flat on top and garnish with chopped scallions. Taste. If you think it needs a little extra oomph, drizzle the bowl with fish sauce or a sprinkle of furikake. Enjoy.

Forget All Your Troubles
by Joan As Police Woman
COMPOSER, SINGER, MULTI-INSTRUMENTALIST

I don't associate food with a specific event. I associate food with every event. The best, all-purpose food that comes to mind is a simple Japanese sweet potato drowned in coconut manna or coconut oil or, best of all, both. It combines sweet, savory, and fatty in ideal degrees. After more than ten years of eating them often, I've yet to get tired of them. Also, they fill you up, unlike chocolate, which just makes you want more chocolate.

I make them whether I am sad or not. But sadness at any level, all of the sadness, is just eradicated by these beauties. They turn sunshiny yellow in the middle and have gorgeous purply pink skin. They're nutty, they're sweet, they're perfect. These sweet potatoes have a built-in olfactory alarm that alerts you when they're almost done—you start to wonder who's baking cookies and then realize it's coming from your own oven. If you do it right, they also have texture, and the skin gets crispy. You are required to eat the skin. Don't even fuck around with not eating the skin. You can't come to my house and not eat the skin.

Roasted Japanese Sweet Potato

INGREDIENTS (FOR 1)

1 Japanese sweet potato

Coconut butter or oil

Salt and pepper

METHOD OF PREPARATION

1. Preheat the oven to 425°F [220°C]. Line a baking dish with parchment paper or foil.

2. With gusto, lovingly stab the Japanese sweet potato with a long, thin blade, remembering you need to preserve the hand that's holding the potato.

3. Roast uncovered for 50 minutes to 1½ hours depending on the size. While roasting, natural caramelization may begin seeping out the holes in the skin—do not fret, simply rejoice. It is ready when it is easily squishable and when the knife slides through the middle with no problem.

4. Slice the potato open and slather on the coconut butter/oil and close it up again so it melts. Season with salt and pepper as desired. Again, the skin is the best part, so don't dare try to discard it.

5. Forget all your troubles.

Sadness at any level, all of the sadness, is just eradicated by these beauties.

A Mess for a Moment by Hassan Pierre

SUSTAINABLE FASHION PIONEER

Alison Riley: Have you ever had a broken heart?

Hassan Pierre: Luckily, no. In the last ten years I have had two serious partners, but I have broken up with both of them.

AR: When you break up with somebody, do you let loose or do you take a little time, or is there no rule?

HP: I have maintained friendships with both of my exes and they're still two of my really good friends. Even though I was breaking up with them—maybe it was a little bit of a heartbreak—there was nothing done in either direction with a malicious intent that would require me to feel like breaking loose or in need of a big release. I am out all the time anyway, no matter what.

AR: Is there any one food you crave when you are feeling sad?

HP: This sounds ridiculous, but peanut butter with melted chocolate and coconut flakes.

AR: That does not sound ridiculous, that sounds delicious.

HP: Anytime I'm sad, that is my go-to comfort food. I melt my own chocolate chips in a double boiler, and then I add some peanut butter, add some coconut flakes, and then I take a banana and dip the banana in there.

AR: Is this the kind of thing you eat over the stove?

HP: Yes. I eat it right over the stove, with a spoon, chocolate gets everywhere, coconut flakes, peanut butter, the whole thing.

It's a one-stop shop and you're done. All better.

AR: *When was the last time you had this?*

HP: Two weeks ago, maybe? I was really missing my significant other a lot, so I decided to eat some of my banana chocolate mess.

AR: *That sounds like it would definitely make you feel better.*

HP: It hits the spot EVERY time.

AR: *Have you ever made that for anybody else?*

HP: No—it is not something I have told anyone either.

AR: *Has anyone seen you eat it?*

HP: One friend on FaceTime has caught glimpses.

AR: *And do you make a portion you can kill in one sitting?*

HP: Yes, I have it down to a science. One banana, I know the amount of chocolate chips and the peanut butter I like, and the coconut flakes. It's a one-stop shop and you're done. All better.

Coasting in on an Empty Tank
by Nicholas Galanin

ARTIST, MUSICIAN

Spring was here, I had just finished community college and planned on driving north, back to Alaska, with my few belongings and my younger brother. It was our first solo road trip together, and we had a map to get us to Canada. This was B.C.—before cell phones—so the copilot map-reading job was important.

We set off, and after several long stretches on the road, my brother and I learned a few things: One, that my prized CD collection had become the most important necessity, a curated collection of punk rock classics, and two, that my budgeting skills were on the optimistic side. We stopped in Seattle to see old family friends before crossing the border, and luckily their mother lovingly snuck an extra sixty dollars into our pockets as we said goodbye.

Right on schedule, we drove toward a small coastal community, set to arrive on the day the ferry would depart for Alaska. On the way, we (I) miscalculated the distance from one gas station to the next and realized we were not only in danger of missing the boat, but it was also likely that we wouldn't even make it to the next pump. The solution was to coast whenever possible and to press the gas pedal only when necessary. The car literally died when we hit the next gas station— we coasted in on an empty tank.

Filling up this thirsty vehicle and feeling relief, I went in to pay... declined... declined... declined. The service station clerk knew I had no other options and kindly offered to rifle through my CD collection as payment for the gas. With no other option, I allowed the unthinkable. All of my favorite albums and compilations became hers. While her greasy gas station mitts continued selecting gem after gem in the form of compact disc, I looked away. I spotted an ancient ATM in the corner of the store. I stuck my card in, knowing that my bank account was at zero. But for some reason the machine spit out a Canadian $20 bill. Amazing. With a three-day boat ride ahead, I had to let her keep the CDs and save the twenty for food. We made it to the boat. We didn't eat well but we ate, and we rationed these meals to get the most bang for our Canadian buck:

Alaska marine highway hot dogs, dry from rolling on the hot dog spinning machine overnight, Jell-O fruit cups full of canned fruit, and, of course, free water with crushed ice. The hot dogs stretched far with free condiments, and the crushed ice was something to chew on.

Fruit Gelatin Cups

INGREDIENTS (FOR 4)

1 cup [240 ml] apple juice

1 cup [240 ml] cranberry juice

One 3 oz [85 g] packet unflavored gelatin

2 cups [280 g] fruit cut into bite-size pieces [apples, berries, pineapple, cherries, peaches, or bananas]

1 tsp lemon juice

METHOD OF PREPARATION

1. Mix the juices together in a mixing bowl. Pour ¼ cup [60 ml] into a small saucepan on the stove. Sprinkle the gelatin over the surface of the juice in the pan. Avoid getting any on the sides, as it could burn.

2. Divide the fruit among four 4 oz [120 g] ramekins, and give them a light tap to settle the pieces into the cups.

3. Bring the juice to a boil while whisking. Boil for 1 minute, then pour back into the reserved juice. Add the lemon juice and stir to cool slightly.

4. Pour the juice mixture over the fruit, dividing it evenly.

5. Place in the refrigerator for 1 to 2 hours, or until the gelatin is set.

To Accompany Pig by Bob Power

RECORD PRODUCER, ENGINEER, MIXER

On the eve of the 2016 election, in excited anticipation of our first woman president, I made a reservation at a wonderful rustic-yet-high-end Italian joint by Gramercy Park in Manhattan.

I asked for one of the few booths along one wall—easier to talk there amid the lively, buzzing atmosphere. In my mind, I imagined all the engaged folks at the other tables as virtuous lefties happily anticipating, as I, a positive social agenda for the next four years.

We were seated around 8 p.m., still too early for any substantive exit polls. While the campaign polls had not been overwhelming, I think I harbored a deep-seated belief that no one as dim and transparent as Trump could actually be elected president. Inside, I felt that it would be akin to someone like Bozo the Clown—or at least Silvio Berlusconi—inhabiting the White House.

When our table was ready, we brought our half-finished martinis from the bar where we had been waiting. And although normally I feel it's degrading to a fine dining experience, we had no compunction about checking our phones every ten or fifteen minutes for any news.

The meal started well enough with a beautifully seared polpo appetizer. These folks have a way with heat—both slow and fast. For the main, I splurged (hey, it's Hillary!) and went for the house specialty: maialino al forno, an exquisitely slow-roasted pig, with oh-so-crispy skin (removed and cooked separately, then replaced on the pig, I believe, for optimum crisping) accompanied by an Etna Rosso.

As more definitive news began to drift in over the course of this wondrous meal, any initial (or later, alcohol-fueled) positive anticipation began to be overtaken by a depressing cloud of doubt, colored in a dull gray-brown, more of a creeping depression than a sudden jolt of bad news; a slow leak from a toilet that, at first, you want to ignore, until the thin layer of brown water is clearly making a statement, slowly spreading over the bathroom floor.

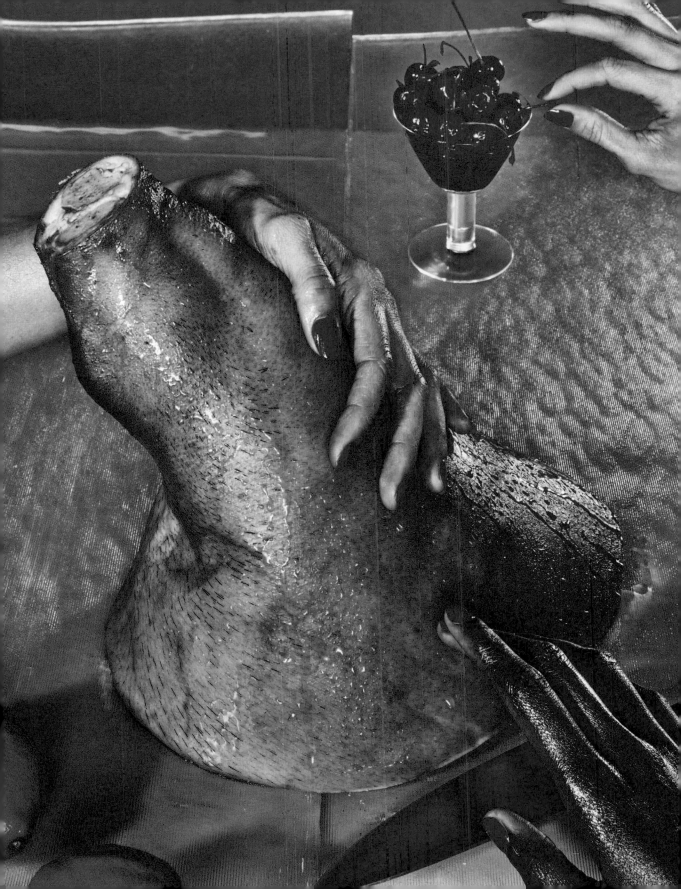

A slow leak from a toilet that, at first, you want to ignore.

By the time we were two-thirds through the main, it was pretty clear that things were not going our way. What a dichotomy ... making our way through this marvelous meal, revealing more delights with every bite and sip, while the other, political, spiritual, and moral side of the scale was dipping in perfect coordination with the rising gustatory end.

Bob's Roasted Cauliflower Side Dish

INGREDIENTS
(FOR 2 AS A MAIN,
FOR 4 AS A SIDE)

1 large cauliflower

2 Tbsp good-quality olive oil

1 large lemon, juiced, rinds reserved

Sea salt

Pinch of cayenne powder [not for heat, just to wake up the flavors]

4 tsp dried oregano

2 bay leaves

1 tsp chopped fresh thyme

1 tsp chopped fresh rosemary

2 Tbsp pine nuts

2 Tbsp chopped kalamata olives

Freshly ground black pepper

METHOD OF PREPARATION

1. Preheat the oven to 375°F (190°C). Line a baking sheet with foil.

2. Wash and break up the cauliflower by hand into bite-size pieces. You can include thicker stems if desired—they are underappreciated. Place in a large mixing bowl. Add the olive oil and lemon juice. Toss. Chop the lemon rind into ½ in [1.3 cm] pieces and add to the bowl.

3. Add the salt, cayenne, oregano, bay leaves, thyme, and rosemary, pinching the fresh herbs to release their flavor. Toss to coat the cauliflower in the seasonings.

4. Spread out the cauliflower on the prepared baking sheet. Less crowding = better browning. Roast for 25 to 30 minutes, until the cauliflower pieces are browned with some blackened spots. If you're lucky, the lemon rind will be a bit blackened. If the cauliflower is very dry looking, drizzle with a bit more oil and/or lemon juice.

5. When the cauliflower has browned, sprinkle with the pine nuts. Continue to roast until the nuts are toasted, 3 to 5 more minutes.

6. Remove the baking sheet from the oven and return the cauliflower and nuts to the bowl. Add the chopped olives and a pinch of freshly ground black pepper. Toss.

7. Let sit for 15 to 20 minutes to allow the flavors to meld. Good warm or at room temperature. Goes well with a fruity medium-bodied Italian red or Beaujolais. Or anything.

The Art of Giving by Money Mark

MUSIC NERD

I grew up in the West Athens borough of Los Angeles, which is South Central proper. And after these fifty-plus years of living in SoCal, it is geographically where my heart still resides.

Vandana Shiva remarks that nature's currency is life, and I tasted life every morning while I walked to school—in the alley between Ainsworth Street and Vermont Avenue, crossing 120th Street, downhill to the gates of West Athens Elementary public school. The first two blocks of this quarter-mile trek were an urban orchard. Let me simply name the fruit trees that were my early morning givers: grapefruit, lemon, kumquat, peach, avocado, pomegranate, apricot, guava, and Santa Rosa plums—those were my favorite! These trees are fewer now, but you can still find them in many parts of LA's southern neighborhoods. Funny. Over the decades the so-called affluent neighborhoods have lost their natural botany to "development," but nature offered unconditionally to a young soul as mine, late for class. I received sustenance for half of the day and a life lesson beyond what was written in books: the art of giving.

My mother did make breakfast for us (I'm the middle son of three boys). Maybe fried eggs over Japanese white rice with refried pinto beans. Or fermented pickles and kimchi. Or cheese quesadillas with handmade corn tortillas. You see, my father was Japanese-American from Hawai'i, and my mother a straight-up Tejana from San Antonio's Southside—though both their birth certificates claim they are "white." My father's chosen first name was Frank. Jitsuro was his Japanese name. My mother was named after the iconic singer-songwriter activist Lydia Mendoza. Yes, I was eating Japanese burritos in the '70s.

Interracial marriage was illegal in Texas, where they were living, so they migrated north to Michigan to start a family. I was born in Detroit, where my mother first heard about powdered milk and other "modern" processed foods. Detroit had pizza and Greek food and Italian food, but eventually my parents set their sights on Los Angeles and a community that opened its arms to them—where they could readily get Asian food products, Mexican spices, and where I could bite into a juicy peach on my way to school. Oh, damn! I forgot my homework!

Guacamole with Pomegranate and Cotijo Cheese

INGREDIENTS (FOR 2)

½ small yellow onion, minced or finely diced

1 tsp minced garlic

1 jalapeño, seeded and minced

2 large or 3 medium ripe avocados, pitted and flesh scooped out

¼ cup [60 ml] fresh lime juice

1 Tbsp kosher salt

½ cup [20 g] chopped cilantro leaves and stems

½ cup [75 g] pomegranate arils

½ cup [60 g] crumbled cotija cheese

METHOD OF PREPARATION

1. In a large mixing bowl, combine the onion, garlic, jalapeño, and avocados. Add the lime juice and salt. Mash and mix gently with a fork, making sure the salt and juice are distributed thoroughly. Taste, and add more salt and/or lime juice as desired.

2. Fold in the cilantro.

3. Transfer to a serving bowl. Garnish with the pomegranate arils and then the cheese. Serve with chips and enjoy!

A life lesson beyond what was written in books: the art of giving.

How to Treat Yourself by Kia Cooks

CHEF, FOUNDER OF KFTP

The lowest point of my life since moving to New York was the summer I left the restaurant Lalito. I think it was actually another chapter of a breakdown in progress, but I had zero mentorship—it wasn't like I was surrounded by elders or other female chefs who might have helped me out and guided me; I was swimming out there on my own, or drowning, before and after I left. Once I was gone, I felt like I'd lost my purpose; I had this whole trajectory planned out for myself that had disappeared. I didn't know what to do with myself.

I didn't want to cook. I realized I couldn't remember how to cook for myself at home. I had spent all my time cooking for fifty to a hundred people every morning and every night and ordering in large quantities. I felt like I didn't know how to shop; I didn't know how to do anything anymore. I was depressed and I was broke. My whole world was asking, *What's next, what's next, what's next?* I was like, "I have only been in New York a short time and this whole thing has been my entire life in a very public way. I don't know what I am doing next, I don't know how to pay my rent. I don't know."

I was struggling for a long time, gliding on this defense mechanism or this protective kind of measure, telling myself this was okay, the universe does things for reasons, blah blah blah. I was trying to contain myself with surface-level affirmations so that I would not burst apart at the seams, only to realize I was trying to prevent a breakdown that I was already in the middle of having. I was lost, for sure.

Then, on August 12, 2019, the Popeyes chicken sandwich dropped. At the time, I lived right around the corner from a Popeyes. It was super cheap but I had no money, and one day I just decided, screw it, I am going to treat myself to that sandwich and see what it's all about. The first thing that blew me away was not the sandwich but the act of getting the sandwich, since I am not used to even having the time to get up and do something, to decide on a whim that I am going to have or do this. That's just not the kind of time I've had before. That felt pretty exhilarating.

And then eating the sandwich—that was the best thing I ever tasted in my life. I had not experienced joy around food in so long before I ate that Popeyes chicken freaking sandwich. I felt like a food critic, tapped in all of a sudden, all about the briny pickle and the batter and the brioche bun. I felt like I knew what I was talking about again because I could engage with food and pleasure and excitement over this fast-food chicken sandwich. It made me feel like a person.

After that, I ate a lot of those chicken sandwiches because it became the thing I would do to treat myself. Before, I'd go have dinner at a friend's restaurant in the city, or buy some wine, or, after a long week when everything went well and no one forgot to order anything, I'd get my check and go get a pair of sneakers on Broadway. I couldn't do that anymore. If anything, I was just celebrating being alive. I was grateful for waking up and sitting down and figuring out how to make money. Once a week, I could get up, get that Popeyes chicken sandwich, and figure out what I was going to do with my life.

I was trying
to prevent
a breakdown
that I was
already in
the middle
of having.

A *Ritual of Hope* by Simon Doonan

AUTHOR, AESTHETE, RABID SOCCER FAN

In the early '80s, on a hot, dry afternoon, I drove my friend Mundo to the doctor to get the result of a biopsy. A weird purple lump had appeared on his neck. It's probably just an ingrown hair.

The doctor was blunt: *This is Kaposi's sarcoma. You have AIDS.*

Can you give my friend a referral to a specialist?

There are no referrals. There are no specialists. This disease is fatal. Are you fellas religious?

We were not religious. We were young and feral and creative and fun-loving. The epic horror of this diagnosis hit us like a ton of shit.

The following day, on the notice board of the Erewhon health food store, I spotted a postcard advertising the Michio Kushi macrobiotic center in West Hollywood. Listed among the conditions that the macrobiotic diet might alleviate was—drumroll!—AIDS.

Mundo went to the center and had a cooking lesson, and then I joined him. We learned about the macro philosophy of George Ozawa. One day, Michio Kushi, the macro guru-in-chief, came to the center and gave Mundo a one-on-one consultation, after which he lit up a cigarette. Mundo was very amused by this.

Mundo died a few months later.

In the 1990s, I read an article that stated that the macro diet is far too radical for AIDS patients, especially people who make extreme changes from, for example, lardy Mexican food (me and Mundo) to ascetic Japanese fare.

Oh fuck!

After cutting out animal protein, Mundo had lost a dramatic amount of weight—
I could have a modeling career!—and his lesions proliferated rapidly. I remember
sitting in a movie with Mundo and his boyfriend Jef. He showed us a couple
of sarcomas that had erupted on his wrist *during the movie.*

For a while I cringed with regret over Mundo's macro interlude. But the truth of
the matter is that Mundo was not long for this world, and macrobiotics was the only
thing that offered him any kind of hope. The process of preparing his miso soup
was a ritual of hope, a simple task that gave him a life-affirming moment in his day.

Macro Miso Soup

INGREDIENTS (FOR 2)

2 Tbsp wakame, soaked in
water for 2 to 3 minutes to
soften, drained, and cut into
strips*

2 cups [480 ml] spring water

*2 Tbsp thinly sliced carrot,
daikon, turnip, or squash*

2 Tbsp miso paste

*½ cup [10 g] finely chopped
kale, chard, or spinach*

1 Tbsp sliced scallion

**Wakame is a dried seaweed
found in many specialty
groceries or health food
stores. The soup is best made
utilizing its unique flavor,
though in a pinch, you could
use a couple pieces of
nori. In that case, add the
nori with your greens.*

METHOD OF PREPARATION

1. In a pot, combine the soaked wakame and spring water.
   Bring to a boil.

2. Add the carrot, lower the heat, and let the broth come to
   a simmer.

3. Place the miso in a small mixing bowl and, using a ladle,
   add a small amount of broth while stirring to dissolve
   the miso paste so it easily mingles with the rest of the soup.
   Add the miso and kale to the broth and stir to combine.

4. Lower the heat and allow the soup to simmer slowly for
   2 to 3 minutes.

5. Serve in a warmed bowl, garnished with the scallion.

The thing about
a pot of beans
is that it can
feed a bunch of
people at once,
in good times
and in bad.

Beans for All Time by Liz Lambert

HOTELIER, DESIGNER

Pinto beans. A heavy-bottomed pot of beans, simmering on the stove in a crowded kitchen, murmurs and laughter, glasses clinking. In a lonely kitchen, a meditation.

Pinto beans were one of the first things I learned to cook when I was young, watching Viola, our longtime caregiver, at the stove. I feel like I have made them a thousand times since then. I made them out at the ranch after my mother's funeral, made them dozens of times for the stragglers staying over after a music festival, made them when the pantry was bare and there was no other way to feed my friends.

Beans were the center of a casual family dinner on Sundays in Austin with my brother, Lou, for years. We would make a crock of brown rice, pick up a roast chicken and some fresh tortillas, and set out bowls of shredded cabbage, slices of radish, chopped cucumbers with salt and vinegar, cut avocado, salsa, and escabeche (and Mrs. Renfro's Chow Chow, if you could find it). But the main event was always the beans.

The thing about a pot of beans is that it can feed a bunch of people at once, in good times and in bad. You can make several meals from one pot, and smash some up to serve on burritos later. You can make them vegetarian, just salt and simmering water, or add a ham hock for a deep umami flavor. Chicken stock is a nice way to flavor the pot. Beans are easy to make once you settle on your preferred method.

Age-old wisdom is that beans must be presoaked overnight, or quick soaked by bringing the pot to a boil, covering with a lid, shutting off the heat, and letting it sit for an hour. There is a current school of thought, however, that you don't need to soak the beans, just begin cooking in cold water. This method will increase your cooking time, but some folks swear it increases flavor. Use a heavy-bottomed pot, with enough liquid to cover the beans by 2 in [5 cm]. Bring to a boil for 5 to 10 minutes, then lower the heat to a simmer.

Once you've got the beans soaked or not soaked and at a simmer, add a rough-chopped onion, a few heads of crushed garlic, a few tsp of chili powder, and salt to taste, and cook for 3 to 4 hours, adding liquid as needed. Add a can of crushed tomatoes, if you've got one, after the beans have softened—highly acidic ingredients like tomatoes will slow the cooking time and toughen the skins, which is maddening, trust me. The beans will be ready when the broth is milky and the beans are tender, and some of the beans have begun to come apart. I like to add a tsp of brown sugar or maple syrup near the end of the cooking.

TO SERVE WITH YOUR BEANS

Pot of brown rice

Chopped cucumbers, set aside with salt and vinegar

Shredded cabbage, also salted, with a spike of vinegar

Chow chow, or pickled things in general

Thin slivers of radish

Sliced avocado

Salsa, escabeche, or jalapeños

Roasted chicken

Stack of good tortillas

Put everything in one bowl, beginning with a bed of brown rice, then the beans, and finish with your choice of the above (chicken and tortillas to the side).

She would fry those potatoes within an inch of their life.

Crispy, Hot, Salty Potatoes by Justin Vivian Bond

CABARET ENCHANTRESS, ACTOR, VISUAL ARTIST

My mom didn't really like cooking too much. But one thing she did love making was crispy fried potatoes. She'd thinly slice potatoes, slice some onion, heat up a skillet with oil or butter, and she would fry those potatoes within an inch of their life: crispy, hot, salty potatoes. There's nothing better! She used to say,

"How about if I just fry us some potatoes?"

If it was a cold day and we were feeling down—or even if we were in a good mood and felt like having something delicious and fun between the two of us. It was true comfort food, but it was also a moment of joyful camaraderie with my mom. To this day, if I feel like I need to cheer myself up, or if I want to show somebody I love them, I say,

"How about if I just fry us some potatoes?"

I'll slice some, heat up the skillet, and the day turns around no matter what. It's not so hard to make, but it's an unforgettable treat!

Crispy Hot Salty Potatoes

INGREDIENTS (FOR 2)

1 Tbsp extra-virgin olive oil

½ medium yellow onion, sliced into thin half moons

Salt

1 large Idaho potato, sliced into thin coins

1 Tbsp unsalted butter

METHOD OF PREPARATION

1. Place a large sauté pan on medium heat.

2. Add the oil. When shimmering, add the onions, and season with salt, tossing a couple of times to coat with oil. Cook for 2 minutes.

3. Place the potatoes in the pan, roughly in a single layer, and season liberally with salt. Cook for 3 to 4 minutes.

4. Add the butter to the pan, and let foam. Cook for another 5 minutes, tossing once or twice to keep things cooking evenly.

5. When the potatoes are well-browned and crispy, turn out onto a plate and devour.

For the Record by Meshell Ndegeocello

I had finished the release cycle of my second album, *Peace Beyond Passion*, and it didn't chart as well as "If That's Your Boyfriend," but there was a cover that did really well. There were some signs the label wasn't sure what to do with me. Madonna's brother, who I loved, had persuaded me he should direct my next video, and I thought I looked like a drag queen. I was pretty unapologetic about my Blackness, my queerness, and my androgyny, but they tried hard to make me more "marketable." Nevertheless, I was feeling really good. I was settling into LA life. The records were sounding good. I was feeling technically on top of my game. I was working on new music.

After my first two albums, David Gamson and I shared an amazing relationship as producer and artist. David taught me how to make music, how to eat well, how to make a good cup of coffee—he exposed me to so many different things. I was always excited to make music with him; it was just a good experience. We went into my next recording assuming that we would be the right combination for the new songs.

We started the record. I wrote "Loyalty," "Bitter," "Fool of Me," and he and I recorded those songs. We had a meeting with the head of the label and a couple other people. We go in, we play the record. That is one of the hardest things to do, and since then, when people ask me to check out something, I refuse to do it when they're in the room. Having been there, it's for the best not to do it with the artist.

I sat in the room, they listened to the music, no one had any sort of facial expression, and they just simply told me that this wasn't gonna work and to find a new producer. The head of the label went over to his stack of *Billboard* magazines and other industry periodicals and asked, "Who has the number one record? Let's call them." No relationship whatsoever. That didn't matter. That was just insulting. I think I got up and walked out of the meeting.

The label wanted a famous producer, and as this was happening, my friend Craig Street was getting kudos having just produced a number of successful albums. I trusted Craig already, so I brought him to LA, we do the whole dance with the

No one had ever said anything like that to me.

label, they're happy, I'm happy, we do the meeting, and we talk about what's left of the budget. After recording with David, and the time writing and just living in LA, there was a fraction of the budget left. That's a whole other story.

We had to make the album really quickly, but it was a great experience, with musicians who became my friends and family to this day. We were in a studio in the Valley that was very brown, like the brown crayon, I remember that. I cooked for the band and made coffee during breaks. It was a nourishing time, and I felt great about the music.

When I handed it in, the label listened and the marketing team told me they "couldn't sell it." The head of the label asked me why I didn't make Black music and told me that I should make a "Black record." No one had ever said anything like that to me. I'd gotten criticism before, feedback and suggestions, but to say that I did not make Black music was really hard to hear. I was crushed. It sent me into quite a spiral, a deeply difficult and depressing summer. The toxicity of that experience contaminated my days for a long time.

By the time it came out, I think the label and I were mutually disenchanted. The album was titled *Bitter*, and it was released with barely any promotion. The good news is that it clarified my own priorities: friendship, musical integrity, people and partners that made me better, clean food and decent coffee. Maybe I wasn't ever going to succeed at being the most marketable and maybe it would cost me fame and fortune, but I would make what I wanted to make.

A *Soft Spot* by Alex Wagner

JOURNALIST

I graduated from college in 1999 and all of my friends, en masse, decided to move to New York, a city that sounded hard as hell to live in. I'd visited Los Angeles one spring break, and here was a city that appeared to have miles of donut shops and innumerable vintage cars, as well as apartments that college graduates could actually afford. I moved there—and smugly noted to all of my New York friends that, though shitty, my apartment complex had a swimming pool. It was good for a while, but then I got another job—and then another, one that requested I relocate back to New York. Two years at that point seemed like a lifetime in Los Angeles, and so the move back east was welcome. There were still college friends available as roommates, and I found my favorite one of them and we moved in together—to what I now recognize as an unbearably shitty, roach-infested dungeon on the as-yet ungentrified Lower East Side. We loved it, I think.

My new job was conveniently located thirteen blocks from where I lived, and, inconveniently, paid me an incredibly low salary, so I was in the habit of packing my lunch for work each day. The Whole Foods Revolution had not yet begun, and so most of my food shopping was done at the bodega or—if I was feeling ambitious—at the "fancy" grocery store on Elizabeth Street, across the invisible poverty demarcation line of the Bowery. Here I could buy sliced whole-wheat bread, which I then used to make sandwiches. I had a soft spot for Italian-style tuna salad, and regularly made a lunch with canned tuna, olive oil, mustard, and black olives on the fancy whole-wheat bread from across the Bowery—which is what I had packed for myself on the morning of September 11, 2001.

That day was the Democratic mayoral primary in New York City, which I remember vividly because I left the dungeon and could not make any calls on my Motorola flip phone as I headed out to vote. I had no television, and there was no Twitter. The only thing I had was an unretrievable voice mail from my mother, who was living thousands of miles away from me, watching the horror unfold on her television at home. A homeless woman on my doorstep told me I'd need to get a refund from my phone carrier for today, "because of the planes." She pointed up to the sky, and I saw the black smoke of disaster curling in the blue—but because this was New York City, where chaos is commonplace,

I assumed it was just something awful but not cataclysmically so, and went on with my day.

I stopped at my polling place on my way to work, I voted in the primary, and I continued my walk to work, sandwich in hand. It was only when I arrived at the office that I realized we were under actual terrorist attack: We were close enough to Ground Zero to hear the screams of people when the towers fell. A few hours later, the street in front of our office was filled with dust-covered traders and secretaries and managing partners walking back uptown, like zombies. I remember the feeling of helplessness and vulnerability that day, but also how hard it was to grapple with the enormity of this hell, to process what was unfolding. Mostly, I remember because while I knew enough to go back to our apartment and pack some things (I knew I wouldn't be coming back for a while), I also couldn't figure out what to do with myself, how to recalibrate for the new reality we had all been thrust into. And so, that afternoon, around lunchtime, back in the dark of that terrible apartment, I opened my tinfoil-wrapped Italian tuna sandwich—a vestige of the old New York from just a few hours earlier—and ate it.

Tuna Salad Sandwich

INGREDIENTS (FOR 1)

5 oz [150 g] canned tuna, drained of oil or water

1 tsp mustard, preferably Dijon

1 Tbsp extra-virgin olive oil

2 tsp chopped black olives

Sliced whole-wheat bread

METHOD OF PREPARATION

1. In a mixing bowl, combine the tuna, mustard, oil and olives. Mix well.

2. Spread on bread and enjoy.

The only thing I had was an unretrievable voice mail from my mother.

Amidst a City Torn Apart by Ulla Johnson

FOUNDER AND FASHION DESIGNER

It was in the time of war, right before the bombing of Belgrade by NATO. My mom and entire maternal family were in Serbia as what I had always been taught was the miracle and magic of Yugoslavia crumbled around them. It had been several years since I had been back. I felt I had to go. Arrangements were made. I was to fly to Budapest and meet persons unspecified who would drive me and several others in a sprinter van through cover of darkness across the intervening miles and countless checkpoints into Belgrade.

In her typical fashion, my mother had not offered me much in the way of detail or encouragement. She had traveled this way herself, seemingly without a moment of fear or worry, and I was expected to do the same. It was a long journey. I cannot remember the number of hours we drove, or how many stops we made, but I do remember I was cold. My denim jacket wildly insufficient, I wrapped myself in whatever other bits and bobs a college girl embarks on such a trip with, which were few and certainly not the most appropriate.

I didn't chat with my fellow passengers much, and instead spent the time thinking of what awaited, how changed my city and family might be. In the end I arrived into my mother's eager arms and was rushed directly to my great-aunt's kitchen. She lived in an apartment that had once felt grand to me, with its proper dining room, fine crystal, and moldings. But the heart of the home had always been Lela's kitchen in the back with a small table featuring a shiny, patterned vinyl tablecloth where she would serve me and my mom and cousins the most delicious of meals—a combination of Austro-Hungarian haute cuisine and Bosnian comfort foods. I believe we ate burek that night—spiced ground meat wrapped in layers of phyllo dough and baked to perfection, and srpska salata consisting of finely chopped tomatoes and cucumbers and onions, and my very favorite dessert, šnenokle (also known as île flottante), a delicious concoction of meringue floating on crème anglaise. We were sad and scared and sorry for all that swirled about us, but this meal and this moment soothed us and, despite it all, laughter and comfort surrounded us in that cozy kitchen, twinkling amidst a city torn apart by conflict and terror.

Šnenokle

4 large eggs

Pinch of cream of tartar

4 ½ cups [1 L] whole milk

¼ cup [50 g] sugar

1 tsp vanilla extract

2 Tbsp all-purpose flour

METHOD OF PREPARATION

1. Separate the egg yolks from the whites. Reserve the yolks. In a mixing bowl of a stand up mixer, beat the egg whites until fluffy, then add the cream of tartar. Continue to mix on high speed until you achieve stiff peaks.

2. In a wide saucepan, heat the milk until it is just under a boil, approximately 200°F [95°C].

3. Using a large tablespoon, scoop egg-shaped dumplings from your egg white mixture and drop into your simmering milk. Cook for 30 seconds on the first side and flip. Cook for another 30 seconds, then transfer to a serving plate to cool. Repeat with the rest of the whipped whites, dipping the spoon into cold water between scoops.

4. Strain the milk to remove any egg white left over from cooking. Return the strained milk to the saucepan.

5. In a separate bowl, vigorously whip the egg yolks, sugar, and vanilla until pale and fluffy. Add the flour and mix well.

6. Add the egg yolk and flour mixture to the milk and cook over low heat, stirring constantly, until the mixture thickens enough to coat the back of a spoon, 5 to 7 minutes.

7. Pour the thickened milk into shallow bowls and float the meringue dumplings on top.

When the Rims Went Down
by Bobbito García aka Kool Bob Love

DJ/PRODUCER, FILMMAKER, AUTHOR, BALLPLAYER

Alison Riley: Do you cook?

Bobbito García: I do cook. I cook, but if you took all the cooking I have done in my life—my whole life—it would not equal the amount of cooking I did in 2020.

In my brain, the pandemic brought me to the "we are at war" place, and I had to survive. I am blessed that my immune system is strong, but I thought, "If I am going to survive this, I need to be as healthy as possible." I was eating 100 percent plant based, and I started jumping rope plus running stairs again as if I were back in college training for b-ball.

I had been toying with being a vegan for probably twenty years. I was introduced to it way back then, and probably in these last two years I had been 70 to 75 percent vegan. I was loving how the food treated my body, and what it meant for the environment, for independent farmers, for pushing forward positive change and anti-corporate, anti-capitalist ideals. Anyway, March 11, 2020, came along and the stay-at-home orders started and I didn't have to be outside or on the road or overseas, opting for something quick and unhealthy. I could control the food narrative on a daily basis, and it became much more plausible to reach that goal of being plant based.

There was a series of deaths in my family in March, April, and May. It was heavy. I couldn't go to funerals, or go hug my mother. And then my son's mother was affected by COVID, so I was cooking for her, bringing her dishes on a little green table, then leaving them outside her door. She wound up being in quarantine for thirty-seven days.

You could combine all the f*ckin' scrambled eggs I've made in my life, all the pancakes—they don't equal the cooking I did that month. I was making her three meals a day, healing foods and soups. Maybe not what my son and I were eating— and what my son eats I don't always want to eat, so, in the course of one day, I was

But the dishes,
the dishes, the
f*ckin dishes.

sometimes making seven to nine meals. The cooking wasn't so bad—it was kind of a joy. I felt like I was helping someone heal, taking care of my son, taking care of myself. But the dishes, the dishes, the f*ckin dishes. The cleaning up afterward, the salt on the counter, the floor has to be wiped up, the garbage has to be taken out more often 'cause there's more food. Endless.

But the event that really crushed me was the week the parks and recreation department took the rims down. In my whole life, basketball has been my source of joy, my safe space, and when the rims went down it felt like the most unthinkable horror film ever. Couldn't go to gyms, couldn't be indoors, only safe if we're outdoors, mask on, distance, but damn, I can't even shoot basketball now . . . F*ck me.

However tempting, I wasn't trying to go to a pizza shop during all this. The nearest shop was a mile and change walk, and I am vegan now, so I started making homemade vegan pizza with sweet potato wraps instead of dough, with the pizza sauce, and the shredded vegan mozzarella, and then I would throw spinach on top, or chop up squash or zucchini, or throw broccolini on top, put my little oregano, sprinkle olive oil, my garlic powder, and everything you'd see at the pizza shop. Well . . . not everything. I can't mess with the red pepper flakes, but everything else, touch of salt and pepper. It would not only feel good 'cause it was a healthy meal but it was that reminder of New York, pizza outside, bugging out, at the shop, walking with a slice with oil dripping out on your shoelaces, and you'd be like . . . "Dag!"

The Simplicity of Congee by LinYee Yuan

EDITOR, *MOLD MAGAZINE*

My cat was dying. For four days, my time was marked by hand feeding, constant fretting, and trips to the vet for bloodwork and a cocktail of pills. On the winter solstice, the longest night of the year, I woke up at 4 a.m. with the urge to make congee. The rice porridge is my ultimate comfort food, a humble bowl that sends warm waves of energy radiating out from my core. My favorite version, made with chicken stock or the leftover chicken bones from a roast, would be a fitting tribute to my poultry-loving cat.

Like its less brothy twin, steamed rice, congee is more a vehicle for other textures and flavors. My ideal bowl would start my day, a warming porridge topped with fluffy scrambled eggs, pillowy pork floss, the sweet and tart tang of soy cucumber pickles, funky chili bamboo, bright green onions, and a generous slick of crispy, garlicky, chili oil. A side of you tiao, a long length of fried dough meant to be torn in two and dipped into the congee or a warm bowl of soy milk, is a nice treat when having congee at a restaurant, but optional.

The warmth and versatility of porridge is a comforting hug that settles the stomach while filling it up. When the world around me seems tenuous at best, comfort can be found in the straightforward simplicity of congee.

When the world
around me
seems tenuous
at best, comfort
can be found.

Chicken Congee for Oski

INGREDIENTS (FOR 2)

1 cup [200 g] short-grain white rice

8 cups [2 L] chicken stock

Salt and white pepper

Aromatics like ginger, carrots, sweet potatoes, and other spices can be used but not necessary

METHOD OF PREPARATION

1. Rinse and drain the rice once or twice with running water to remove any impurities.

2. Add the rice and chicken stock to a large pot. Bring to a boil over high heat, partially cover the pot, and turn down the heat to medium-low to maintain a simmer. Stir occasionally to make sure the rice isn't sticking together or to the bottom of the pot.

3. The congee is done when the rice has bloomed and incorporated the stock, about 1½ to 2 hours. It should have the consistency of oatmeal.

4. Season with salt and white pepper (if you have it!) to taste. Serve with a mix of savory, crispy, umami toppings of your choice.

Indestructible Pea Soup by Brian Lehrer

HOST, *THE BRIAN LEHRER SHOW*, WNYC RADIO

I tend to eat and cook very simply and am not the person to turn to for recipes, believe me. In fact, I recommend that you skip this page and go on to the next person.

For those of you who chose to read on anyway, here's another thing about me that's not worth knowing: In the early days of the pandemic, I was figuring out how to safely get food into my apartment, like everybody else, but then I had this dental problem—I'll spare you those details—that resulted in an extraction and the beginning of the process for an implant. (Take this as another opportunity to flee if you'd like.)

Dental work, of course, is not the most fun you'd ever have to begin with, but in the pandemic, I was less concerned about some dumb tooth that I could get replaced than I was petrified by sitting with my mouth unmasked and wide open for someone to mess around in for an hour or so who was not from my household, and had no vaccine passport for me to ask for yet. I wondered about that thing I had just learned about how N95s don't work all that well on health care workers if they're not individually fitted. Did this solo practitioner dental office know how to do that? At least I wasn't in Texas, I thought at the time, where dentists might have the right to exercise personal freedom and not wear a mask at all. They are very pro-choice about what to be pro-choice about down there, if you know what I mean.

It all turned out fine. But it put me on soft food for the transition, and gave me a craving for split-pea soup. News flash: The split-pea soup in a can you might have grown up with gives you a month's worth of sodium. So I consulted with a friend who knows how to turn on a stove better than I do, and got a recipe for a simple and smooth, deliciously thick split-pea soup. Best served really hot, and don't skimp on the pepper if pea soup is usually too bland for you.

A good thing for me about split peas is that they are virtually indestructible. They can't break, like those eggs I thought I was clever getting delivered rather

Dental work, of course, is not the most fun you'd ever have to begin with.

than going into a store. Also, like with many soup bases, you can add veggies or whatever you like to help make it a meal. Chopped carrots are one common choice. Also, you can make pea soup thicker or thinner—I go for about as thick as it can still be called soup—depending on how much water you add. First sauté some curry powder in olive oil over low heat. Then stir in some crushed garlic, add the water and peas, and liven it up with that sprinkle of fresh ground pepper to taste. Between the pea soup and the automatic permission to have a lot of ice cream that comes with a soft-food diet, you can still have fun eating during your next dental recovery. And if you need another recipe, just let me know and I'll ask another friend. Personally, I'm just about out.

A G&T for the Down & Out
by Gabrielle Hamilton
CHEF, OWNER OF PRUNE RESTAURANT

When I was sixteen, I moved to NYC with $230 in high school graduation gifts and a large jar of loose change, and I survived on this for months until I could find a job. I swiped handfuls of ketchup packets from McDonald's to make spaghetti sauce. I bought canned sardines at the bodega for 35 cents each. And wherever there was an advertised happy hour with free hot food, I laid my stacks of quarters onto the bar and ordered two bottles of the cheapest beer they had. I always left a separate stack of quarters to tip the unsmiling bartender, but even so, he seethed his disdain as he set the little paper plate in front of me that came with the qualifying two-drink minimum. Those complimentary Buffalo wings and that watery beer were sometimes my only meal in a span of days.

I still love a can of sardines—with Triscuit crackers and Dijon mustard—and am not above an occasional Buffalo wing when the craving strikes. But my down-and-outs now require a bracing and crisp gin and tonic. I just can't be consoled by piss-water beer anymore.

It's a 50/50 gin-tonic ratio. Keep the Tanqueray in the freezer so it pours like syrup. Use solid ice cubes that won't water down the "medicine." Keep the tonic refrigerated, too, and tally the giant squeeze of lime as part of the 50 percent mixer, not the 50 percent gin, obviously. Cold, crisp, effervescent, and pretty hefty, it's a real mood elevator. If you bring the drink to your lips for a first sip and notice that in your distracted despondency you forgot to peel off the little barcode sticker on the hunk of lime now floating in the ice, consider it extra good luck, as I do.

Gin and Tonic

INGREDIENTS (FOR 1)

3 oz [90 ml] Tanqueray gin, kept in the freezer

2½ oz [75 ml] Fever Tree Refreshingly Light tonic water, refrigerated

¼ juicy lime, fully squeezed into the drink

Solid cube ice

METHOD OF PREPARATION

1. Combine all ingredients and stir. Serve.

I just can't be consoled by piss-water beer anymore.

If Martha Stewart Only Knew!
by Richard Christiansen

FOUNDER OF CHANDELIER CREATIVE, FLAMINGO ESTATE, OWL BUREAU

I was fishing with friends on a commercial fishing trawler in the Long Island Sound, heading toward Block Island. The water was so choppy, and the cell service was, too. Suddenly, I got a message that Martha Stewart would be coming over for dinner.

We pulled the lines in and scrambled to get back to land. The house was a disaster after a string of parties, and Martha would be aghast at its condition. The trawler and its brooding, whiskey-smelling crew with their huge leathery hands dropped us off in the harbor near my place in Montauk, and we swam ashore. Makes me laugh now to think of it, these gruff Montauk fishermen watching this gaggle of gays scrambling ashore to clean the house for Martha Stewart—high alert on the high seas!

Back at home, we frantically cleaned from top to bottom, throwing anything and everything into the cupboards and closets with wild abandon, just beating the clock as Martha finally arrived. Always game for conversation and cocktails, we chatted up Martha late into the night. For dinner, we prepared the fresh sea bass we'd caught. Of course, Martha said that it needed some salt.

Exhausted from the day with the evening successfully behind us and Martha out the door, I was ready to relax. Looking for a T-shirt, I opened the bedroom armoire only to unleash an avalanche of dirty dishes, bread loaves, mail, casserole pans—you name it—from among the clothes. If Martha only knew!

Suddenly,
I got a message
that Martha
Stewart would
be coming
over for dinner.

Simple Roasted Striped Bass

INGREDIENTS (FOR 4)

Four 6 oz [170 g] striped bass fillets, skin on

Kosher salt

Extra-virgin olive oil

METHOD OF PREPARATION

1. Preheat the oven to 300°F [180°C].

2. With paper towels, pat the fillets dry. With a very sharp knife, score two small slits in the skin of each piece. Do not cut from edge to edge or cut too deep.

3. Preheat a large nonstick or well-seasoned cast-iron pan over medium-high heat. Generously season each fillet on both sides with salt.

4. When the pan is hot, add some olive oil. Place one fillet skin side down. Press lightly with a spatula to brown the skin. Repeat with the other fillets.

5. When the edges of the fish start to brown slightly, slide the entire pan into the oven. After 8 to 10 minutes, check your fish. The sides should be a nice white while the top is just slightly opaque. Remove the pan from the oven and, using a stiff spatula, slide under the skin and flip the fillets. Let them rest in the pan for 5 minutes to ensure cooking on the flesh side; when tested with a meat thermometer, the fish should reach 120°F [50°C].

6. Transfer to a paper towel–lined plate to absorb leftover cooking oil.

7. Serve with lemon wedges or a simple salad.

Scared & Horny Sandwich by Fran Tirado

WRITER, PRODUCER, COHOST OF *FOOD 4 THOT*

Coming from a Chicana-Boricua diaspora, you'd think my parents would've passed more of our Latinx culinary tradition down to me. Yet, all I really got was this sandwich "recipe." As the oral history goes, my parents (then twenty-two and twenty-three) were dirt broke and living together for the first time in a one-bedroom apartment. Fresh off their honeymoon, their lives were turned upside down with the news of their first child (moi), who they were neither emotionally nor financially prepared for. The first night they spent together as a newlywed couple in their apartment, they ate a cold rotisserie chicken sandwich with a baguette, avocado, and lime—a meal that cost less than $10 at most grocery stores.

This simple sandwich became my favorite growing up, so much so that I would request it on my birthday. Now, I return to it as a comfort food when I am scared, horny, or both, which is often. I ate this sandwich the day my first boyfriend in New York broke up with me. It was my first relationship in four years and I had uncharacteristically put myself out there only to be totally rejected (though he did later call to tell me to get tested because he might've given me gonorrhea). That day, I'd also managed to eat shit stepping off an MTA bus in front of a crowd of pedestrians, badly bloodying up my knees and palms. New to the city, without friends, bandaged up, and crying alone in my first dirt-broke apartment, I wondered if I could handle the pressure of making it on my own. Heartbroken, I made myself this sandwich to feel something familiar. It satiated all my needs and staved off my scaries/horniness 'til another day.

I return to it as a comfort food when I am scared, horny, or both, which is often.

Rotisserie Chicken Sandwich

This is my version, updated slightly to accommodate my fanciness.

INGREDIENTS (FOR 1)

1 fresh French baguette

2 Tbsp unsalted butter

Whole-grain mustard

2 oz [50 g] sharp Cheddar cheese, thinly sliced

½ ripe avocado, minced

Coarse salt and freshly ground black pepper

Red pepper flakes

2 oz [50 g] soft goat cheese

1 handful baby kale

¼ store-bought rotisserie chicken, shredded

½ lime

Do I really need to "follow instructions" for this recipe, you may be thinking? It's a sandwich, not rocket science. Where I am not a deli essentialist, I am a Virgo moon and do have a specific way of putting this together if you care to follow along.

Slice open the baguette lengthwise with a serrated knife and separate into two parts. Removing the butt of the baguette, cut the desired portion of bread (I personally go for a hand-sized sandwich). Spread half the butter onto both sides of the bread slices and set on either side of a cutting board. On one side, spread the desired amount of mustard, layering the Cheddar cheese on top. Also on that side, spread avocado and sprinkle with salt, pepper, and red pepper flakes. This specific layering prevents the bread from absorbing the moisture of the avocado and creates optimal flavor combinations with Cheddar-mustard and Cheddar-avo.

On the other side, spread the goat cheese and top with the baby kale. Pile as much rotisserie chicken as can fit onto the kale side, then squeeze the lime half (more or less) onto the shredded chicken until evenly moistened. Again, this creates optimal taste combos, and kale prevents the lime from absorbing into the bread. Using a spatula, flip the avocado side carefully onto the chicken side. Melt the remaining butter in a skillet over medium-low heat. Transfer the sandwich to the skillet and grill until golden brown, or a little more. Flip and grill until the Cheddar cheese has completely melted.

If exceedingly scared/horny, this sandwich is just as good skipping the grill and eaten cold.

Security Pizza by Becca Blackwell

PERFORMER, WRITER

When I was little, I thought that girls who were fat didn't get molested. I had a paper route, so I had cash and I figured out how to order pizza. I would keep pizzas under my bed so I could eat them, get fat, and be safe.

And since I was assigned a vagina at birth, I would spend the rest of my life thinking I was fat since so much of a woman's value is based on her body and her attractiveness to men. Add that to being a soft-looking butch, and I never could find any sense of power internally. I had conflicting systems running inside of me. I felt more masculine, but I never felt like a man. All of which is probably why I never felt like I fit in. But eventually queerness will expand, my place will appear, and we will all be LGBTQIABCDEFGHIJKLMNOPQRSTUVWXYZ.

Here's how I get pizza now:

Preheat the oven to 450°F [230°C]. Basic crust recipe: In a large bowl, mix one ¼ oz [7 g] package of yeast, 1 cup [240 ml] of warm water, and 1 tsp of sugar together. Let sit until creamy, 8 to 10 minutes. Then add 2½ cups [350 g] of flour, 2 Tbsp of olive oil, and 1 tsp of salt. Beat with a hand mixer or a wooden spoon until smooth. Let sit for at least 5 minutes. Roll out into rounds or whatever shape you like pizza in.

My personal favorite topping is a poor man's pesto, which is 1 bunch of parsley and 1 bunch of cilantro blended with garlic, salt, olive oil, and pepitas (or almonds or walnuts work if you're rich). If I have fresh Parm, I'll throw it in. I put a thick layer on the dough and then add sliced Brussels sprouts that I have precooked in olive oil and garlic. Put a little of that Parm on and shove it in the oven. If I've got dough left over or want another pizza, I use any leftover pesto and then I do a chorizo and broccoli rabe (I always add fresh garlic to the broccoli rabe when cooking). Put some of that fresh Parm on and goddamn. Each pizza needs about 12 to 15 minutes depending on how crispy you like it. Salt is your friend.

Eventually,
queerness will
expand and
we will all be
LGBTQIABC
DEFGHIJKLM
NOPQRSTUV
WXYZ.

Staples by Rachel McKibbens

POET, WITCH, MAMA

Any time one of my uncles had a court appearance, my grandmother would listen to the guttural ballads of Chavela Vargas as she stirred a cauldron of pintos over the stove. Instead of singing along, she'd chase each lyric with "MY BOY! MY BOY! MY POOR BOY!" Melodrama, the first ingredient.

A staple for every Mexican family, beans are shamefully overlooked due to their simplicity, but it is in the careful ritual of their preparation that you notice the soft pings of love and grief ricocheting off the heart's interior. If you've grown up in a house of the habitually incarcerated, you know it has its own kind of weather: rising steam from the boiling water humidifies the kitchen, peeling the wallpaper eventually. It coats the kitchen windows where children, wallowing in their freedom, can draw primitive little :(with curious fingers—telegrams of grief for each passerby. Uncle Vinny's sentence for gun possession meant a plastic bag slit open, dried beans cackling onto the linoleum tabletop. The silence we held as we sifted out the misshapen rejects or small stones became the second ingredient.

Over the years, as each sentence elongated a son's absence, my grandmother taught me the hand is the best measuring cup, tears an adequate response to both cash bail and severed onions. When Uncle Phillip got clipped for his third strike, it was a slow pot of beans that soothed our family. Breakfast, lunch, and dinner. Tiny jalapeño bits and garlic were added once Gilbert's parole officer found out he OD'd. Locked up again for addiction. More salt, 'til the water becomes gray. Cayenne for the daughter he never met.

I now own a restaurant in Upstate New York, far from the streets of Southern California where I grew up. My grandmother's beans are on the menu, an automatic side dish to our tacos. Often, they come back to the kitchen, untouched, and I scrape them into the trash, wash the dish, and keep it moving. But every once in a while, someone will ask, "Who made the beans?" and I come out to greet them, because it's always someone who gets it. "They taste like my grandmama's beans!" or "These remind me of my favorite beans from El Pollo Loco! I had to meet the person who made these. You from Cali?" And always, always, I say, yes,

I'm from Santa Ana. Mi barrio. My grandmother taught me how to make them. But she died with the tamale recipe. Never shared it. She needed something to stay hers.

Spicy Pinto Beans

INGREDIENTS (FOR 4)

½ cup [70 g] diced onion

½ cup [60 g] seeded and diced jalapeño

2 Tbsp minced garlic

2 Tbsp garlic powder

1 Tbsp cayenne pepper

One 1 lb [455 g] bag dried pinto beans

Salt

METHOD OF PREPARATION

1. Fill a large pot with water to about 2 in [5 cm] below the rim. Add the onion, jalapeño, minced garlic, garlic powder, and cayenne to the water, but do not add the salt. I mean it, do NOT add the salt! Bring to a boil over high heat.

2. While waiting for the water to boil, empty the beans into a bowl and sort out any stones or oddities. Add the sorted beans to the boiling water, lower the heat, and allow to simmer until the water darkens and becomes broth-like. Stir occasionally.

3. The beans will take a couple of hours to become tender. Optionally, add salt to the water once they are soft. If added earlier in the cooking process, the beans will become tough. I am a salty bitch and salt the hell out of them. Your call!

4. DO NOT DRAIN THE WATER.

5. Serve in a bowl with a large flour tortilla, folded into a quarter.

Melodrama, the first ingredient.

Mother of Invention by Jacqueline Woodson

AUTHOR

Chicken . . . again.

My mom couldn't cook. She tried. We didn't starve. We circled the table every
evening not so much dreading what was put down in front of us, but with
an ennui four kids in Brooklyn by way of the South should never have to bring
to the dinner table. I always chose the window seat. There was a gutter drain just
outside of it, and this is where so much of my dinner ended up. Once, as a child,
I put liver and onions in my pocket and later had to lie away the cause of the grease
stains. Lumpy grits. Thick, undercooked Aunt Jemima pancakes, pink-boned
chicken, cube steaks like chewing gum, dry and blistered porgies—the list went
on and on. My sister, younger brother, and I were underweight. My older brother,
existing on a diet of mayonnaise sandwiches, junk food, and bodega heroes, was
not. Still, we survived. I credit a lot of that survival to my best friend Maria's
mother. Maria lived three doors away and her mother pulled magic out of her
refrigerator and kitchen cabinets—rice and chicken stews (arroz con pollo),
pigeon peas with bits of beef, deep-fried pastalitos, chicken soups—yes, it was
still chicken—but it . . . *wasn't*.

And we survived too because my grandmother joined us in Brooklyn when
we were still young and took over the cooking. A Southern woman to the core,
my grandmother was both a gardener and a chef. She and my mother turned
our backyard into a world of milk crates sprouting collards, lettuces, tomatoes,
cucumbers, and herbs. My mother planted an apple and a pear tree that, all these
years later, still bear fruit. Our world became Southern fried chicken and fried
sweet potato pies. It became collards cooked with smoked turkey wings and
macaroni and cheese casseroles. It became homemade ice cream and ambrosia,
pancakes from scratch with caramelized bananas. It became a world I walked
into and discovered my own love of silent time in the kitchen, figuring out how
to turn the old into new (chicken seemed to always be on sale somewhere in the
Bushwick of my childhood and because of that, we ate it—a LOT!).

Now when I want to revisit that childhood—from my grandmother's kitchen to
Maria's mother's—this is the dish I find myself making.

A Black Girl's Puerto Rican Chicken Stew

Here's the thing about sofrito—make a whole bunch, freeze it in ice cube trays, and pop a few cubes out to season just about anything you're cooking—from beans to greens to meats.

Sofrito

INGREDIENTS (1 CUP)

8 garlic cloves, roughly chopped

1 large yellow onion, cut into eighths

1 red bell pepper, seeded and cut into quarters or eighths

1 green bell pepper, seeded and cut into quarters or eighths

1 bunch cilantro, rinsed and roughly chopped

½ cup [120 ml] olive oil

2 Tbsp salt

METHOD OF PREPARATION

1. Put the garlic in a food processor and pulse until finely chopped.

2. Add the onion, bell peppers, and cilantro and pulse until finely chopped, almost like salsa. Add the oil and salt and process briefly until incorporated.

3. Reserve or freeze.

Chicken Stew

2 Tbsp olive oil

6 to 8 bone-in chicken thighs

Salt and freshly ground black pepper

1 yellow onion, roughly chopped

2 garlic cloves, chopped

3 to 4 Tbsp sofrito (recipe precedes)

1 bay leaf

2 Tbsp cumin

1 Tbsp onion powder

1 Tbsp garlic powder

1 Tbsp dried oregano

1 tsp paprika

1 tsp turmeric

1½ cups [360 ml] chicken broth

One 6 oz [170 g] can crushed tomatoes (NOT with basil— I sometimes make that mistake!)

1 Tbsp tomato paste

½ cup [120 ml] water

METHOD OF PREPARATION

1. In a Dutch oven over medium, heat the olive oil. Season the chicken with salt and pepper, add to the pot, and brown on both sides, then set aside on a plate (if it seems like a lot of oil left in the pan, drain a little off).

2. In the same pan, sauté the onion and garlic for about 2 minutes.

3. Add the sofrito. Cook—if frozen—until melted. If fresh, cook for about 3 minutes. Add the bay leaf, cumin, onion powder, garlic powder, oregano, paprika, and turmeric. Sauté for a minute but don't let the spices burn.

4. Add the chicken and its juices.

5. Add the chicken broth, crushed tomatoes, and tomato paste. Bring to a boil.

6. Lower the heat, sample and adjust to taste, and cook for 40 to 50 minutes, partially covered. If the liquid looks low, add the water.

7. For the last 15 minutes or so, cook uncovered over low heat. You want the chicken falling off the bone.

Zigni to Warm My Heart by Raul Lopez

CREATIVE DIRECTOR OF LUAR

My friend's mom, Florina, invited me to Easter brunch at her home during a very difficult moment. Two days before, I lost my cousin to a sudden illness. Florina told me I had to come, and promised she would make something that would warm my heart after all the pain.

Around her table, Florina explained that, as a child in Sudan, her mom would make zigni, an Eritrean dish, for Easter day. Florina is Egyptian and Sudanese. She said she recreates the foods from Africa and her childhood because they are rich in flavor, spices, memories, and love. Zigni was all of those things; it was iconic in flavor and unforgettable in my heart.

Zigni

INGREDIENTS (FOR 4)

2 Tbsp [30 ml] canola oil

1 lb [455 g] onions, chopped

1½ Tbsp berbere spice

1 lb [455 g] stew meat (beef is traditional but chicken thighs or lamb shoulder works), cubed

⅓ cup [80 g] tomato paste

1 cup [240 ml] water

One 16 oz [455 g] can crushed tomatoes

2 hard-boiled eggs, peeled and quartered

METHOD OF PREPARATION

1. Place a pan large enough to hold the meat over medium-high heat. Add the oil and onion and cook until lightly browned.

2. Add the berbere and cook for 2 minutes.

3. Turn the heat up slightly and add the cubed meat. Stir well and cook for 5 minutes.

4. Add the tomato paste and cook for 1 minute. Add the water, then add the tomatoes.

5. Turn the heat down to low and cover. Simmer for approximately 2 hours or until the meat is tender, stirring occasionally.

6. Serve, garnished with the hard-boiled egg.

Joy and Relief by Alba Clemente

THEATRICAL DESIGNER

As a Southern Italian, I know that food is the cure for everything. Food cures the body and the soul. Food is called for in happy celebrations and sad occasions. Sitting at a nicely set table in front of a good meal—preferably with family members or friends—is always a joy and a relief.

As a mother, I also know that once your children are fed, most of the work is done—for that day. But another one starts soon after. And another. But there was not an evening, raising our four children in New York City and having a pretty busy life, that we didn't have dinner all together. I loved them, but I have to say, it was a relief when they all went to college and I didn't have to cook seven days a week.

Pasta alla Puttanesca

INGREDIENTS (FOR 2)

Salt

¼ cup [60 ml] extra-virgin olive oil

2 garlic cloves

1 Controne, Calabrian, or cayenne chile pepper

10 kalamata olives, pitted

2 Tbsp capers, rinsed if salted

15 cherry tomatoes, or one small can whole peeled plum tomatoes, drained

4 oz [115 g] dried spaghetti

METHOD OF PREPARATION

1. Place a large pot of water on the stove. Salt generously and turn to high heat.

2. Place a sauté pan over medium heat, add the olive oil, and warm. Lightly crush the garlic and mince. Add the garlic, chile pepper, olives, and capers to the pan. Cook for 5 minutes.

3. Add the tomatoes and cook for an additional 15 minutes.

4. While the sauce simmers, cook the pasta. When the water comes to a rolling boil, add the pasta and lightly stir to separate the noodles. Cook according to the package instructions. Dried spaghetti usually takes 10 to 12 minutes.

5. When the pasta is cooked, strain. Don't rinse the noodles! Add the noodles to the sauce and toss for a few minutes.

6. Serve immediately.

A *Dish to Hold the Love* by Damani Baker

FILMMAKER

I come from a family of chefs. Louisiana is in my blood, food, and heart, but I learned to cook from my father, Prestin, who was from Denver, Colorado, and knew food was care. The type of care that meant sitting still, trout fishing at San Pablo Dam with packed lunches of fried bologna sandwiches, generic store-brand soda, and Fritos. After church, roasted chicken with canned beans and skillet cornbread.

On December 7, 2005, Prestin Levi Baker, my father, transitioned as lung cancer took over his body. December 7 is also my birthday. After his funeral, where the piano player played a few bars of Earth, Wind & Fire's "Fantasy" per my request, while sitting in his home, food began to arrive. The faces of every elder and ancestor whom I could remember rang the doorbell not to stay, not to speak too much, but to leave a dish knowing it would hold the love they felt for us in every bite. Their faces looked like the ones I remember in Geismar and Denver; they looked like the faces of both of my grandparents. They were faces of my mourning family, smiling at me like my father sitting on the shore, smiling at me without speaking, letting the sunflower seeds fall beneath us.

Aunt Shirley's Red Velvet Cake

INGREDIENTS
(FOR ONE TWO-TIERED
9 IN [23 CM] CAKE)

Nonstick cooking spray

2 large eggs

2 cups [480 ml] vegetable oil

1 cup [240 ml] buttermilk

3½ tsp vanilla extract

2 cups [400 g] granulated
sugar

2 tsp Hershey's unsweetened
cocoa powder

1 tsp baking soda

Pinch of salt

2½ cups [350 g] all-purpose
flour

¼ cup [60 ml] red food
coloring

8 oz [230 g] Philadelphia
cream cheese, at room
temperature

½ cup [115 g] butter, at room
temperature

One 1 lb [455 g] box
confectioners' sugar

Splash of milk

½ cup [60 g] chopped pecans
[optional]

METHOD OF PREPARATION

1. Preheat the oven to 350°F [180°C]. Spray two 9 in [23 cm] cake pans with nonstick cooking spray.

2. In a large bowl using a hand mixer, or in a stand mixer, beat the eggs, oil, buttermilk, and vanilla on medium speed until combined. Add the granulated sugar, cocoa powder, baking soda, and salt and beat until fully incorporated.

3. Add the flour, little by little, followed by the red food coloring. Mix until completely smooth.

4. Transfer the batter to the prepared pans, splitting evenly between the two.

5. Bake for 20 to 25 minutes, until a toothpick inserted in the center comes out clean. Let cool in the pans, then remove from the pans and transfer to a cooling rack.

6. In a large bowl with a hand mixer, or in a stand mixer, whip the cream cheese and butter together until smooth. Slowly add the confectioners' sugar and milk. Finish with three-fourths of the pecans, reserving the rest for decoration.

7. Frost the cooled cake, then sprinkle with the reserved pecans.

Spread Peanut Butter, Not Pain by Ron Finley

THE GANGSTER GARDENER

Alison Riley: So the reason you don't have any one story about a low point is because these aren't the memories you're trying to carry forward.

Ron Finley: I mean, I thought and thought and thought . . .

AR: No! Good for you if you're not carrying it forward.

RF: I'll tell you, though, I went to a Tony Robbins event and, you know, they have you walk on the coals, and people are crying. In one exercise, they want you to feel the pain, to get into the pain that you have. And I was trying— trying to feel the pain. I called over one of the event people and said I didn't think I was doing it right. She said just to be calm and feel whatever came. And I was trying to get into it, to find some pain. I mean, I am Black and I grew up in America; I got to have some pain. When it was over, and people shared all these horrible stories, I realized I am not holding on to any of that, I don't have that kind of pain. Seeing that, hearing that, it just let me know: I am not feeling it because I do not have it. I don't take that pain with me.

AR: I aspire to that.

RF: But what really came to mind is peanut butter. Peanut butter has always been my go-to when times were lean.

AR: Do you prefer it any way in particular?

RF: I make a hell of a peanut butter sandwich. Get some grilled challah with sautéed bananas, sautéed strawberries, PB, and then some strawberry jam. So you got this hot fruit with this hot, grilled soft bread.

AR: Ooh, grilled bread.

RF: You know, you go to places and you say I want the bread *grilled* and they give you *toasted*. People don't know the difference between grilled and

I am not holding on to any of that, I don't have that kind of pain.

toasted. I don't want it toasted. Toasted gets hard. Grilled still keeps some of the soft.

AR: Are you a chunky peanut butter person or do you like it smooth?

RF: I like mine smooth. It just spreads better. The peanuts, you know, they wind up . . .

AR: Ripping the bread!

Grilled Peanut Butter and Strawberry Jam Sandwich

INGREDIENTS (FOR 2)

1 pt [300 g] strawberries, sliced

2 ripe bananas, peeled and cut into coins

1 tsp sugar

Pinch of salt

1½ Tbsp butter

4 slices challah bread

Peanut butter

Strawberry jam

Note: you'll need to have a hot grill fired up or a cast-iron stove-top grill pan ready to go.

METHOD OF PREPARATION

1. In a bowl, gently mix the sliced strawberries and bananas with the sugar and salt.

2. Place a sauté pan that will comfortably fit all the fruit over medium-high heat. Add the butter. When it starts to bubble and foam, add the strawberries and bananas. Toss a couple of times to coat the fruit with the butter. Turn up the heat to high and cook the fruit until just tender, tossing or stirring frequently. Turn out the cooked fruit onto a plate and keep warm.

3. Place the challah slices on a hot grill or grill pan; you should hear an audible "hiss" when it hits. Let it cook on one side for 4 to 5 minutes, until you start to see browning on the edges. Using a spatula or tongs, take a peek and if you have solid grill marks, flip to the other side. Let cook for just 1 to 2 minutes. The goal here is to have a nice char on each face but steamed and soft throughout the interior.

4. To assemble, spread a layer of peanut butter on one half of your sandwich. Add a healthy dose of strawberry jam on the other half followed by a layer of the fruit. Top with the peanut butter slice of bread. Cut in half and serve warm.

My Favorite, Then and Now by Thundercat

BLACK MICHAEL MCDONALD IMPERSONATOR

I guess this would all go back to the days when my friend Austin Peralta was still alive. Right before he passed, I got a chance to take him to my favorite restaurant, Yoshinoya. It was somewhere my dad used to take me when I was a kid and it just kinda stuck with me throughout my whole life (it's still my favorite restaurant). Austin and I spent a whole lot of time together and were always picking at each other over things, be it big or small. He would challenge my reasoning on things all the time and made things interesting and fun. One drunken night, after a show somewhere in Hollywood around 3 or 4 a.m., we tried to find some food. He suggested tacos, and I got a bit excited about that, but then I was like, "Naw, let's go to Yoshinoya," and he was like, "What the hell is that?" I proceeded to tell him how important this restaurant was to me and we made the decision to go there.

My dad would get me the chicken bowl when I was a kid, but I would always get the beef bowl and the chicken bowl mixed up because I thought that the name of the bowl I was always eating was a beef bowl, as that was the name of the franchise. Austin wanted to see what all the fuss was about, so he insisted that he get the same thing I was getting. This was the order:

Extra-large chicken bowl
– extra chicken
– no veggies
– extra sauce

We took it back to my apartment but didn't wait to get in the house to eat. I didn't like the idea of eating outside on Crenshaw Boulevard at 4 a.m. with this crazy-ass piano player on a damn skateboard, drunk as hell, in front of my apartment complex, talking loud like we were still at a concert, waking up all the neighbors while we argue about Ron Carter. But this is one of my fondest memories of Austin. He died shortly after that at his young age. So all I can do now is remember the crazy skateboarding post-gig 4 a.m. dinner with one of my best friends ever to live and die, the great Austin Peralta.

Ceviche on the Stoop by Angelo Baque

CREATIVE DIRECTOR AND FOUNDER OF AWAKE NY

Angelo Baque: So, COVID. May. I felt like I hit a low point. I had been home alone, I don't think I had seen anybody, and I got really sick and tired of pasta and tacos. That was all I made for the first two months. Both of my parents are from Ecuador and the national dish is ceviche. Specifically, we're from the coast, from a city called Manta, and it's a huge port town, so if you're there you go to the malecón, the oceanfront, and you see big tuna being unloaded at like five in the morning. Culturally, how I grew up was: a lot of fish, a lot of seafood. If it swims, we ate it—that was the rule of thumb in our household.

My mother is the matriarch of the family, and her ceviche, her fish and shrimp ceviche, is incomparable. I have yet to taste anyone's, from restaurants to home cooking, five-star meals, whatever, of all the places I have been to, that compare to my mother's ceviche. I guess I was always afraid to even ask her to teach me, or to attempt, cause I thought she'd shut it down and kick me out of the kitchen.

I was missing my mom, I was alone, I was single at the time, and in all my feelings of deep patheticness and loneliness. It just dawned on me that I think I could do this, and I decided I was going to teach myself how to make this ceviche.

I was thinking, how's this any different from making salsa? I've seen my mother cut the limes, the onions, the cilantro. Some of her secrets are using adobo and salt and pepper, but there are no measurements, all this is just like making a potion. It's instinct and knowing how long to leave the shrimp in the lime and, of course, what's key is that you have to squeeze the limes, everything has to be from scratch, you can't use bottled lime juice.

There's a form of ceviche where you lightly boil the shrimp—less than like two to three minutes—and there are some dishes where the fish or the shrimp is cooked just by the lime, by the citrus. I prefer that—I don't like the flash boil because I feel like it overcooks the shrimp. That's me. It's the texture.

I worked myself up for it. I cut twenty-four limes. My mother put me to work as a kid, showing me this is how you squeeze limes, this is how to clean a shrimp.

It was like a form of meditation and therapy. Squeezing the limes and cleaning the shrimp—that is the memory of food. Not even the dish itself. It's all in the labor. Everything else is really easy.

Alison Riley: Do you have a recipe or do you just work off memory?

AB: Honestly, it's so simple and it is really about one's own personal taste. The key is getting that base right and letting it sit in that base. You gotta add a little filtered water to break down some of the acid 'cause sometimes straight lime juice is a little too acidic. But it's just salt, pepper, garlic, if you're feeling a little spicy throw in some jalapeños. What's key is the red onions, tomatoes, and the cilantro, which you add at the very end when you're ready to serve. You don't want that sitting in there.

AR: How was it?

AB: The first time, it was decent. And then over the summer, when people started to get more comfortable with seeing each other outside, I brought a bowl of ceviche to a friend's stoop in Bed Stuy to share. Everyone kept teasing me that I had a secret girlfriend who was cooking my shrimp ceviche for me. I ended up taking four or five batches to the stoop over the summer for special occasions.

This dish will always be connected to my family. When we got to eat ceviche, it was a treat, like a reward, because it is so labor intensive. To do it right, it is about a forty-eight-hour process. When I was in the second grade, I brought ceviche to elementary school for lunch, and I was so proud. This little white girl looked at me and said, "Your food stinks," and I was so embarrassed. I was embarrassed of the food, and though at the time I didn't realize it, I was feeling embarrassed of my culture—of being Ecuadorian. I thought, "You know, she's right. She's eating a fucking peanut butter and jelly sandwich, and that's what I should be eating." And I didn't really understand the layers of that trauma until I got older.

Now, being an adult and making the ceviche myself, and sharing that with all types of people—my friends, white, Black, brown, Latino—on my friend's stoop in Bed Stuy and everyone really enjoying it and appreciating it, I was like having this second life with this dish.

The real reward was making it for my aunt and my uncle and my mother, and they approved of it. They loved it. You know, if someone really loves you, they'll make you chifles, the plantain chips, which again, is not rocket science, it's just a pain in the ass 'cause you gotta thinly slice the platano. I made them chifles.

AR: Damn.

AB: Yeah! When I went to LA, I made chifles and ceviche for my friends and they were blown away 'cause they'd never had it like that. You know, in LA the culture is people eat ceviche on top of a tostada, but I cook white rice and the chifles and serve it on a bed of lettuce, in a little bowl. You scoop whatever's on the bottom with the lettuce. That's how I was taught. I got to pass on that ritual to my friends and share that with them. That's it.

An Overflow of Love and Plumbing
by Andrew Tarlow

RESTAURANT OWNER

The thing about always being busy is that it can often keep you from noticing the things that actually matter, and, in my case, it took a really disgusting situation to wake me up to what I couldn't see all along.

I met my wife, Kate, in June of 1998, the same month that my partner, Mark Firth, and I signed the lease on a then seventy-year-old dining car that was one block away from our loft on the South Side of Williamsburg. Kate was a new server at the Odeon, where I was bartending at the time, and, between working nights at the Odeon and the demo and construction at the diner every day, there would have been no chance for our new romance if she hadn't been more than willing to move in with us and join the rhythm of our days. She was an enthusiastic member of our team, if not very skilled in construction, and she made herself valuable by cooking us lunch down the street every day.

Days became weeks, weeks became months, and finally the big day had come and it was time to open the diner on New Year's Eve 1998/1999. That time is such a blur to me, waking up early for garbage pickup, prepping food all day for dinner service, working long services, and then closing the restaurant at 3 a.m. every night. Kate, Mark, our chef Caroline Fidanza, and I were there for it without a day off for many weeks, and those days were full of fun and joy, but no time for reflection.

One night, a couple of months into the winter of 1999, Kate, Mark, and I are in the full swing of another crazy service on a Saturday night when we get a shout from the kitchen that the plumbing is overflowing in the basement. I remember Kate was wearing a long gray skirt and these crimson velvet sandals that she had bought for herself in the South of France the year prior. She came barreling down the stairs to help with the septic mess and when she got to the bottom, her feet came out from under her and she landed fully in the mess, sandals fully trashed, but with a huge smile on her face, laughing as she looked up at me.

It was in that moment of filth and chaos, and maybe failure, that I fully felt the depth and breadth of her devotion to me. It hit me like a punch to the gut and tears came to my eyes. The weight of her young love knocked me out, and if not for a couple inches of sewage on the floor of the basement, I don't know how long it would have taken me to wake up to what was right in front of me for so many months. Twenty-three years have passed since that night and we have many more businesses and four children, and a very full life—good thing that running restaurants is ripe with daily mini-disasters so that too much time can never pass without getting that punch to the stomach to remind me of the love that is all around me.

Coq au Vin

INGREDIENTS (FOR 4)

Red table wine, enough to cover the chicken

6 bone-in, skin-on chicken legs and thighs

1 bunch of thyme

6 bay leaves

¼ cup [60 ml] extra-virgin olive oil

1 large onion, chopped

2 tsp garlic, minced

2 medium carrots, peeled and chopped

4 stalks celery, chopped

Salt and freshly ground black pepper

4 oz [115 g] bacon or salt pork, diced

2 Tbsp unsalted butter

2 large leeks, halved, cleaned, and cut into ½ in [12 mm] half-moons

12 oz [340 g] cremini mushrooms, thickly sliced

METHOD OF PREPARATION

1. Pour the red wine into a baking dish, add the chicken, and let soak. Make a bundle of herbs with the thyme and bay leaves and add to the wine. Marinate for at least an hour, up to 24 hours. Remove the chicken from the marinade and pat dry. Strain and reserve the marinade and herb sachet.

2. Preheat the oven to 250°F [120°C].

3. In a large pan, heat 2 Tbsp of the olive oil and cook the onion, garlic, carrots, and celery with pinches of salt until soft and translucent. Remove from the pan and reserve.

4. Season the chicken liberally with salt and black pepper. Add the chicken and bacon to the same pan, and brown on both sides. Reserve the crisped bacon on a warm plate.

5. Remove the chicken from the pan and wipe out the pan. Return the chicken and its juices to the pan and add the wine, herb sachet, and onion, carrot, and celery mixture. Cover the pan, transfer to the oven, and cook for 30 to 45 minutes, until cooked through. Reserve the chicken and strain the cooking liquid, discarding all the solids.

6. For the sauce, return the cooking liquid to the pan and cook down further, until slightly thickened. Remove from the heat and add 1 Tbsp of the butter to make the sauce glossy and creamy. Add the chicken to the sauce and keep in a warm place.

7. In a separate pan, warm the remaining 2 Tbsp olive oil and remaining 1 Tbsp butter and sauté the leeks and mushrooms until soft. Season while cooking with salt and pepper.

8. Combine the sauce, chicken, leeks, and mushrooms on a serving platter and garnish with the reserved bacon.

9. Serve with warm rice or buttered noodles.

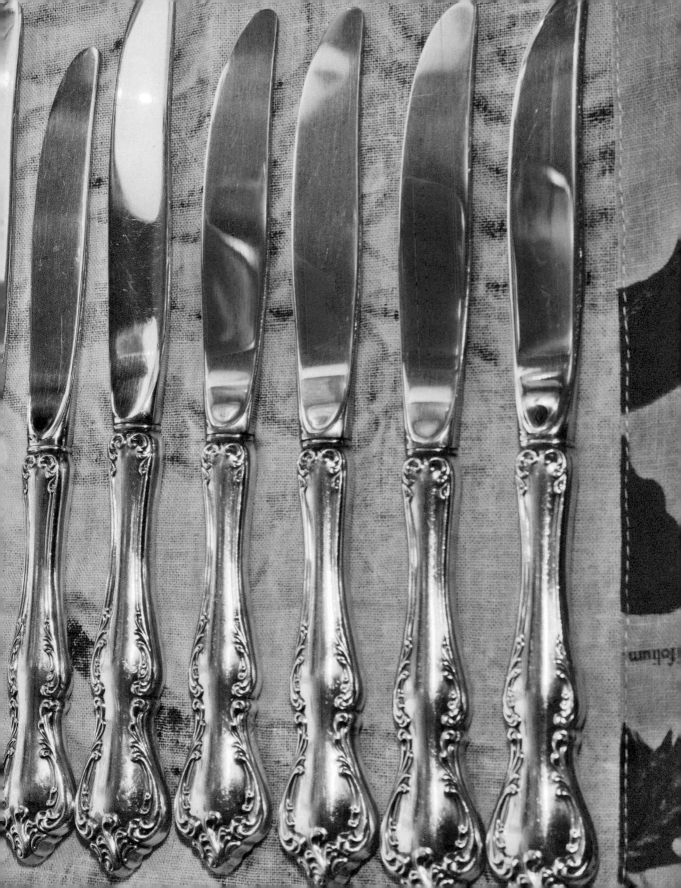

How do you hold your weight?

Eighth Grade Memory Dance by Kyle Abraham

DANCER, CHOREOGRAPHER, ARTISTIC DIRECTOR

Close your eyes and envision a memory of your thirteen-year-old self.
How do you hold your weight?
Is your spine upright or hunched?
Remember the smell of the lunch room?

From those memories, soften both knees, and rotate your left hand and left foot.
Raise both shoulders and allow your right forearm to rise slightly;
leading from the back-hand side of your right wrist, open your right forearm
and step back on your right leg while curving/hollowing out your torso.
Send your left ring finger to the vulnerable space where your clavicle meets
your throat.
Your head shifts back to the left, diagonally.
Both knees turn inward, parallel.

Right knee and foot rotate onto the ball of the right foot.
Left fingers leave the throat and present a "stop" gesture to the back, diagonal
of your body.
Right knee turns in, while staying on the ball of the right foot. At the same time,
your right forearm inverts to have your fingertips pointing toward the floor.
Shift your left scapula toward your right and let that ripple through the right arm.
Right arm continues until your right fingertips are closer to your right eye and
your left ring finger touches your bottom lip.
From there, drop your head, and let your full body react (like a wave or ripple
through your spine).
Step forward on your left foot (in parallel).

With tension in both hands, push both hands past your waist.
Keeping the left hand where it is, allow your right shoulder blade to send your
right forearm to a 90-degree angle.
Leading with the right fingertips, sink in your head and chest, have your
left fingers meet your right in the center of your sternum, and close your eyes
(if you've opened them).

Keeping your eyes closed, continue to soften your sternum—hollowing out as much as you'd like . . . softening the knees in support (and to create more space for the back to settle).

Come back to your eighth grade memory.
How did you hold yourself?
How did a loved one hold you?
What did they smell like? What did their room smell like?
Keeping that memory present, and keeping your eyes closed, straighten both legs.
Keep your left hand connected to your sternum (allowing the fingers to spread more and the weight of your palm to lend heat and support to your heart and chest).
Slowly straighten your right arm.
Open your eyes . . . and feel present.

You show up at your concert with no pants on. How could you forget your pants?

De-Humiliating Muffins by Emily King

SINGER, COMPOSER

The invitation came.

"Come to the show tonight!"

Anita Baker sold out at Radio City Music Hall.

Of course I would go. I grew up listening to Ms. Baker on WBLS, the Quiet Storm. There was no voice like hers. So very identifiable.

My managers let us in the back way. We had VIP passes. "This is cool," I thought. A legend. Something I can talk about. Something I can remember. Great seats too. What are the chances?

Alicia Keys sat near us. Yeah, this IS cool. Anita sang and swayed through the night, sounding like a master of her voice. Soaring. Highs, lows. Restraint. My best friend Tierra was with me. Two-thirds into the concert, my manager shows up in the aisle shouting something. He seemed excited and nervous. From the look of his lips he was saying, "She wants you, come with me now!"

Just like that I'm eight years old at the talent show with adrenaline racing through my entire body. "Please, no." I thought.

"Nooooooo . . . no no no." I shook my head frantically. "I don't know her music. I don't know the songs!" I shouted.

"It's okay!" he replied. "Just sing the blues."

"What?" I winced. I didn't even know what that meant, but it somehow was enough to convince me.

I am not accustomed to improvising at other people's shows. I never do it. Even my own show is mapped out to the minute.

"Come now, she asked for you!" he said again. I looked at Tierra. She looked at me. Next thing I knew, we were both backstage.

"She's going to call you on after this song," the sound man said loudly and handed me a pair of in-ear monitors so I could hear the band.

"No monitors on stage," he said.

"Great," I thought. I pushed them into my ears and prayed that the music gods would feed me the right sounds.

There is a dream, a reccurring dream that performers have. You get called for a gig. You have to sing an Italian aria. You don't speak Italian and you've never sung opera before. The curtains rise, go! You show up at your concert with no pants on. How could you forget your pants? Boom, spotlight . . . you're up, kid, hit it! You slept in and missed the first half of the biggest show of your life and make it just before the ending; the audience hates you for being late. You open your mouth and nothing comes out . . . showtime, go!

The beauty of this dream is the waking up part. You sigh with relief and shake it off as you get up and make your morning coffee. "Ooof, thank heavens, it wasn't real." *sip*

This, however, was not that. Unfortunately. Radio City Music freaking Hall, sold-out show. My hometown. People I know and might recognize. Anita Baker, the legend. She calls me on stage to sing a verse of her song that I had never heard before. I repeat, NEVER HEARD BEFORE. Yes, I listened to WBLS but always casually and never with the intention of learning the words.

I looked down. Still wearing pants. "OK, you can do this, Em."

I'm on stage. I look at her, she points at me. "You take the verse!" she says and walks off the stage. I repeat, WALKS OFF THE STAGE. Holy shit, that is cool but please come back, Ms. Anita Baker. Come back please. It's me now and the band and a song I do not know and I can't hear the music because there is no sound in my in-ear monitors. No sound. A quiet stage. A full house. Trust me, I tried shaking myself awake several times.

"What now, Em?" I looked out at a confused and nervous audience. I called upon my show biz angels for help. "Are there chords playing?" "Try to hear them." "Talk to the audience. Say something!" I looked out into the crowd and shouted, "Give it up for Anita Baker!"

Crickets.

They'd been giving it up all night and now I was taking it all the way down. And I had no more planned material. I can remember trying to sing "ooohs" and "ahhhs" and two-stepping a lot. Clapping, trying to get the audience to clap. I was literally one step away from juggling. Juggling would have been better. This is bad, I thought. Really bad.

Is she coming back? I looked around. Am I left to finish out the show? What was I thinking? What was my manager thinking? You don't say no to Anita Baker is what we were both thinking. Why didn't I say no? I longed for that "no" now. I looked at the band. "Can we turn back time on this one please guys? To like three minutes ago so I can run out the back door? Thanks!" Then suddenly, in my peripheral vision, an angel appeared to rescue me from this very real nightmare. Ladies and gentlemen, Ms. Alicia Keys!

I applauded loudly and so did the audience. My heart exhaled in relief! A nervous, panicked gratitude. The crowd goes wild. A professional has arrived to save us both from entertainment hell! Thank the gods. The band was still playing the song I had been expected to sing. I looked over at Alicia. Did she know the words? Maybe not. But you'd never know it. "That's how you do it," I thought. "A fucking pro."

When the night was over, so was I. I was DONE. "This will never go away, Em. This is going to last forever on the internet," I told myself. Shame and humiliation just a click away for all of eternity, enjoy! A reminder of the night I let down R&B and Anita Baker and myself. Upset with my inability to say "No." Upset that this recurring dream had made its way into my dimension. Some glitch in the system, I suppose.

We stuck around after the show. I desperately looked for redeeming qualities in the night, knowing I'd soon be home reliving my agonizing mistake. Rewind.

Play. Cry. Rewind. Eat ice cream. Cry. Repeat. And then suddenly, through the crowd, there she was. In her dress. Sitting in a chair side stage. Changing out of her heels into a pair of Uggs. "That's how you do it," I thought. "A fucking pro."

I caught her attention. "Thank you for coming," she said. "When I was young, people did that for me." She smiled and I smiled back, simultaneously thanking and apologizing to her. "I'm so sorry, Anita." She didn't seem bothered or upset. She slipped on the other boot and kept moving. Did she know what happened up there? Of course she did. I was grateful.

I went home, lay in my bed, and tried so very very hard to fall fast asleep.

Banana Walnut Chocolate Chip Muffins

INGREDIENTS (FOR 6 SMALL MUFFINS)

¼ cup [55 g] butter

2 very ripe bananas, mashed

1 large egg

½ cup [100 g] sugar

1 tsp vanilla extract

1 cup [140 g] all-purpose flour

½ tsp baking soda

Pinch of salt

½ cup [90 g] chocolate chips

½ cup [60 g] toasted walnuts

METHOD OF PREPARATION

1. Preheat the oven to 375°F (190°C). Grease six cups of a muffin tin or line with paper liners.

2. In a small microwave-safe bowl, melt the butter. Pour the melted butter into a medium mixing bowl and add the mashed bananas, egg, sugar, and vanilla.

3. In a separate bowl, mix the flour, baking soda, and salt.

4. Add the dry ingredients to the wet ingredients, add the chocolate chips and walnuts, and mix well. Divide the batter among the prepared muffin cups.

5. Bake for 15 to 20 minutes, or until a toothpick inserted into the center comes out clean.

Thank you.

Many people helped to make this book what it is, but the contributors who gave their time, heart, and memories to this project certainly top the list. Thank you for your effort and thoughtfulness; I am proud and grateful to have each of your stories in here.

A huge and heartfelt thank-you to all the colleagues, agents, assistants, and gatekeepers who made it possible to extract each of these stories and tolerated my many, many, many emails and thinly veiled pleading.

My immeasurable thanks to Jamie Thompson for the trust, guidance, and belief in my ideas all these years. Thank you to Vanessa Dina and everyone at Chronicle for their expertise and enthusiasm.

Thank you from the bottom of my heart to Grant Cornett, whose ability to find the optimism in melancholy and vice versa has kept my sensibility company for over twenty years. Your work was as much a point of inspiration as execution for this project.

To Ben Wagner, to whom I, almost literally, owe everything: From the title to the precision and rigor of all these pages, thank you for turning so much raw material into organized beauty.

To Ryan McLaughlin, who spilled a gallon of milk on the floor mat of his car during the hottest week of the summer and the week he tested these recipes, crystallizing our theme into perfect form: Thank you. I am lucky to have your friendship and talent on my side.

Thanks to Amy Wilson and Maggie Ruggiero for their skills and invention. Props to Ella Loudon for being the kind of person who plants her face in a cake with such style and confidence.

Thank you to Sam Wagner for the patience, efficiency, and actual skills to make some words into a book.

To Denny Agassi for your assistance, insight, and overall brilliance. You made this whole experience more fun and the result more potent.

Thanks to Sarah Hsia for making sure I dotted my i's and crossed my t's and didn't send myself to jail.

To Mariel Cruz, I can't thank you enough for your unmatched support, unflinching feedback, and unfailing friendship. Thank you to Emily Bernstein for being the best. And thank you to all the brainstormers and true believers who helped make this list of contributors what it is: Jason Rodgers, Paul Hamann, Jane Gladstein, Tchaiko Omowale, Kelly McCabe, Pam Nashel, Nicole Hegeman, Suzi Jones, Kim Holly, Avery Willis Hoffman, Jack DeBoe, Andrea Clemente, Mason Pettit, and Weyland Southon.

Thank you to the people who kept and keep me going: David Riley, Joan Dolan, the Hothans, Tanya Lofgren & Delia Kurland, Sarah, Sam & Alex, the Thompsons, Ultimate Neighbors, John Mahoney, Tedd Patterson, the Johnson/Miners, Amee Gray, Rachel McPherson, Leila Zimbel, Rebecca Meek, the P floor, the Hurins, Samanta Fonseca, Erica Turett, and Mali Sicora. Thank you to the loves of my life, Solomon and Atticus. And to Meshell, whose recipes are the cure for so many of my life's disasters: Thank you, I love you beyond words.